CW01652087

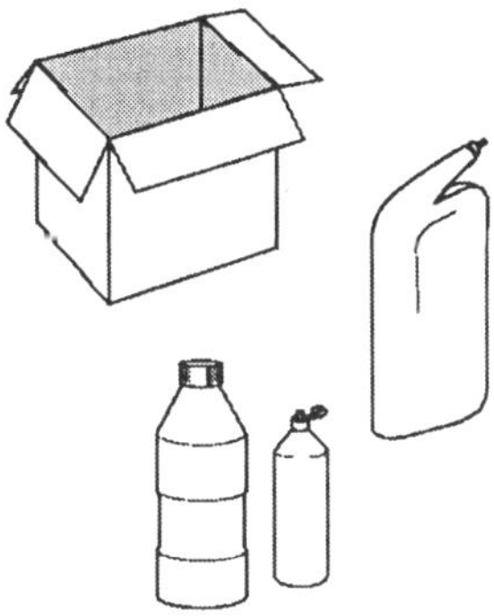

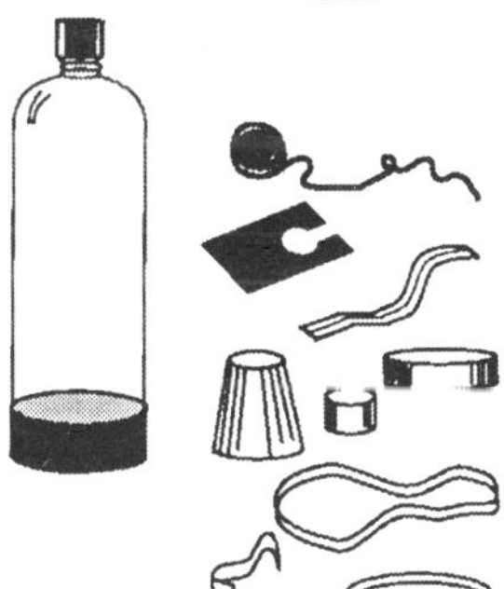

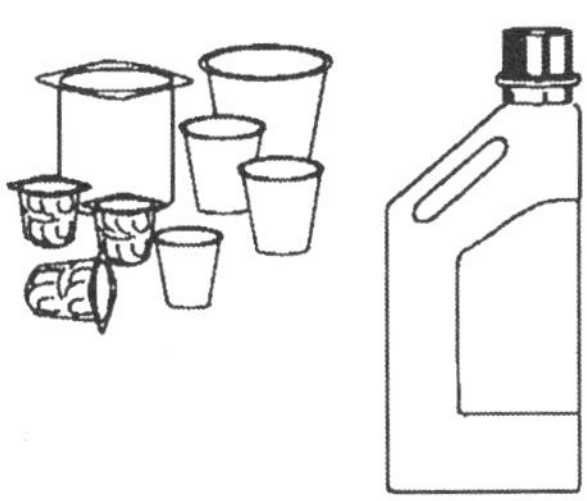

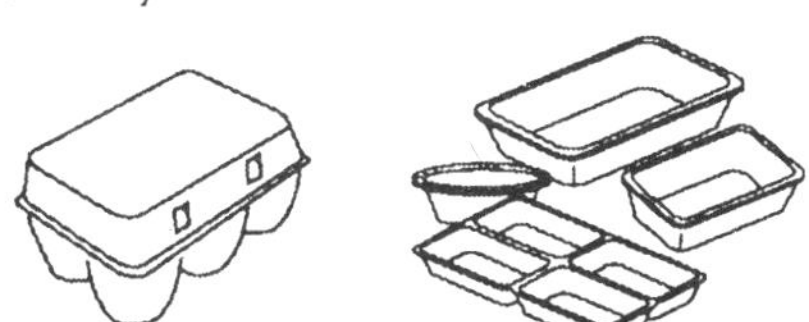

To all those who wish to do more with less.

250 WAYS TO REUSE PACKAGING

Copyright © Michael Harris 1992

British Library Cataloguing-in-Publication Data
A catalogue record for this book is available from the British Library
ISBN 0 9519956 0 X

First published 1992
by
Desert Island Press
9 Wootton Way, Cambridge, CB3 9LX

All rights reserved. No part of this publication may be reproduced, stored in any retrieval system or transmitted in any form or by any means, electronic, mechanical, photocopying, recording or otherwise, without the prior written permission of the publisher. Whilst every effort has been made to ensure that the information contained in this publication is correct and accurate, neither the author nor the publisher can accept any responsibility for any errors or omissions that may have occurred. No liability shall attach to the authors, the copyright holder or the publisher for loss or damage or injury of any nature suffered as a result of reliance on the reproduction of any of the contents of this publication or any errors or omissions in its contents.

This book is sold subject to the condition that it shall not, by way of trade or otherwise, be lent, resold, hired out, or otherwise circulated without the publisher's prior consent in any form of binding or cover other than that in which it is published and without a similiar condition including this condition being imposed on the subsequent purchaser.

Editorial consultancy by Josephine Warrior
Design and production by Yew Design
Printed in Great Britain by Piggott Printers Ltd

ABOUT THIS BOOK

Current estimates indicate that each UK family spends about £660 a year to pay for the original cost of packaging and its subsequent disposal. That works out at about £20,000, in an average lifetime, for every one of us, spent on packaging. It's a lot of money but surprisingly packaging only accounts for a small proportion of all the waste produced in the UK. Litter, however, is highly visible in our towns and countryside and it's mostly packaging. Nevertheless we should remember that at the end of the day only people can produce litter – packaging cannot throw itself away!

Most of us reuse the odd packaging item: we soak paint brushes in jamjars, store buttons and pins in margarine tubs, and cakes in an empty biscuit tin. These are all good ways to make more use of something that would otherwise have been thrown straight in the dustbin. Unfortunately that's exactly what most of us do with enormous quantities of these useful items: throw them away, even though we've paid for them as part of the product.

Over the next few years we're likely to see an expansion in the use of refillable, 'bring-back', containers which will reduce waste and be much better for the environment. Yet while there are many negative aspects to mass consumer packaging, there are also some very clear benefits. Modern packaging materials and techniques have dramatically cut the energy required to process and distribute a very wide range of goods and they are also a key factor in reducing rates of food spoilage in the industrialised countries to around 2%, compared with anything up to 50% in the third world.

One thing is certainly clear about packaging, however, and that is that with little more than enthusiasm and a pair of scissors, it's very easy to make really useful products from what normally goes in the bin.

This book is a collection of 250 ways to reuse packaging, laid out according to packaging type. It is not, of course, complete but we hope that it is comprehensive, in as far as any such book can be, in its coverage of the major types of packaging materials and containers which are common today.

All the ideas can save time, money and help the environment. Some will save you a lot of money: you won't have to buy a purpose-designed product when an ordinary packaging item will do just as well. And anything else you did buy would most likely be surrounded in yet more packaging, which you would then throw away...

So help break the circle now – and save money too – by reusing these valuable materials and containers in all sorts of ways in addition to the one for which they were 'designed'. The more you get into the habit the more you'll be amazed at the clever uses you'll come up with yourself!

CUTTING AND USING MATERIALS

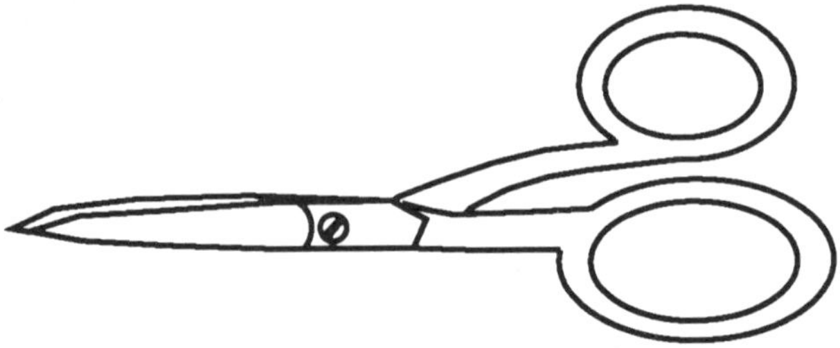

Most of the uses described in this book require only a few seconds' work, and none more than a few minutes, to put into practice. Everybody can easily do them but children should, of course, always be supervised by a responsible adult. The essential tools required are a sharp knife and a pair of scissors. These will do for most of the book and anything else, such as a glass cutter, small hacksaw, office stapler, etc, is mentioned in the relevant section. A supply of wire coat hangers, or any type of stiff gardening wire, will also come in handy for some sections of the book.

Plastics and cardboard can usually be cut quite easily with a knife or scissors. Mark out the area to be cut first and to save time draw up paper cutting templates for things that you are likely to make frequently. When using a knife, be sure to hold the item firmly, cutting away from, not towards, you. Smooth off any sharp edges with a file or abrasive paper: if an item will be handled regularly, for instance a plastic bag tidy, even soft plastic cut edges can graze your hand if you're not careful.

The easiest way to pierce holes in most plastics is with a hot metal spike. Heat the metal only to the point where it will soften and push through the plastic, not so it will set fire to it. Be sure to do this in a well ventilated place and hold the item firmly and well away from anybody else. Melted plastic can cause very bad burns so take every precaution to ensure safety.

An alternative method for piercing plastics and other thin materials, like tin plate, etc, is with a hammer and nail: support the container with a piece of wood, directly under the area to be pierced, and sharply hit the nail with the hammer.

Finally do remember that non-food packaging should never be used for anything that involves direct contact with food and drink, and anything that is, must of course be thoroughly cleaned and rinsed first.

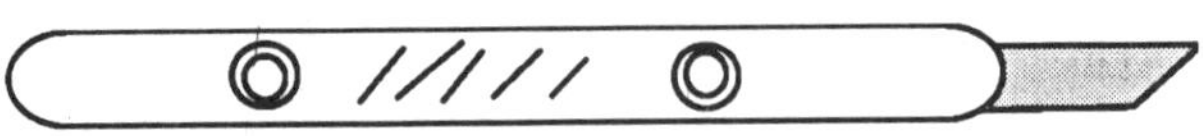

MILK AND LARGE PLASTIC CARBOYS

Bulk liquid products are often sold to the domestic consumer in a variety of large plastic containers. Distilled water, vinegar, milk, vegetable oil, washing up liquid and car engine oil are just some of the items packaged in large carboys, often up to 4-5 litres in size. These are eminently reusable but do remember that food and drink must only be put into containers that were previously used for this purpose. The moulded-in handles make carrying and handling very easy and all sizes can be used either complete or cut down. Try using them for...

TOOL BOXES

Cut away the top part of the bottle leaving a handle attached. (With most containers this usually entails cutting down the

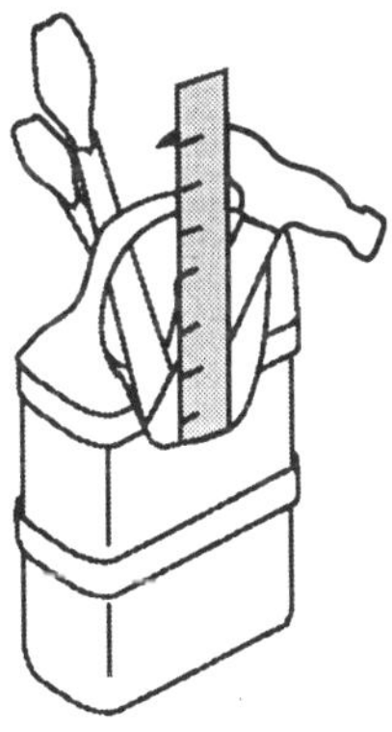

back of the neck to the depth you require as illustrated.) These container tool boxes are perfect for carrying around tools while working on the move – mending fences, decorating, bicycle and car repairs, and so on.

HERB WINDOW POTS

The bottom half of plastic milk jugs are ideal for growing larger quantities of herbs on the window sill. Cut off the top just below the handle.

BOAT BALERS

Cut the bottom off any carboy to make a light flexible baler which can be secured to the boat with a line tied to the handle.

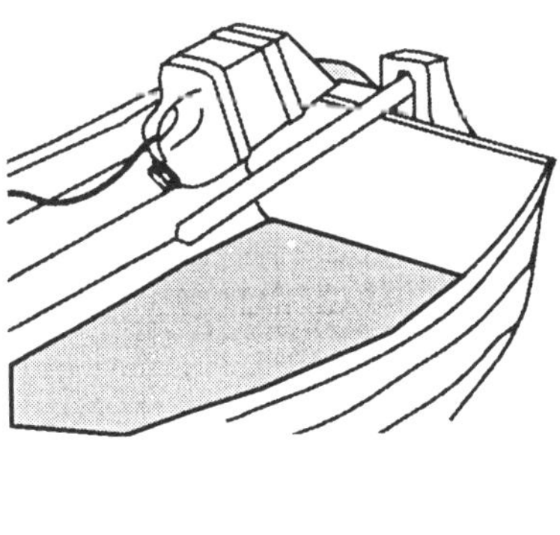

FLOWER POTS

Cut down any suitable container for a variety of useful flower pots. The plants won't mind the shape so long as the size is adequate.

SCOOPS

Cut off the base diagonally, from just below the handle to the opposite bottom corner, to make a useful scoop for dry goods like fertiliser, animal feed, compost, plaster, etc.

GENERAL PURPOSE HOLD-ALLS

Nails, screws, glues and pastes, shoe polishing, cake icing kits – there are an endless number of ways to make use of these containers and save time and trouble by keeping bits and pieces together in one place. Select an appropriate size and cut down as for a tool box.

PICNIC SQUASH JUGS

Large plastic milk containers are great for filling with squash and other drinks for picnics. The handle makes pouring much easier than from ordinary bottles and milk containers are light and easy to flatten afterwards.

GROW BAG WATERERS

Save yourself some work and make sure your grow bags don't dry out by using milk containers as water stores. Cut off the bottoms of two containers and push the necks into the compost through slits cut in the bag between the plants. Steady if necessary with a couple of sticks on either side pushed into the bag. Keep topped up with water and adjust the flow, to keep the compost moist but not flooded, by loosening or tightening the container's caps.

LARGE ICE-MAKING CONTAINERS

If you need a lot of ice, fill a milk container four-fifths full with water and put in the freezer overnight. Wrap in a polythene bag and crush with a mallet or a block of wood. If the container doesn't split, cut open with scissors to extract the crushed ice. Keep any surplus bagged in the freezer for when you need it. Freezers work more efficiently when full, so if stocks are low, bags of ice will help fill the space and save you energy.

COOL PACKS

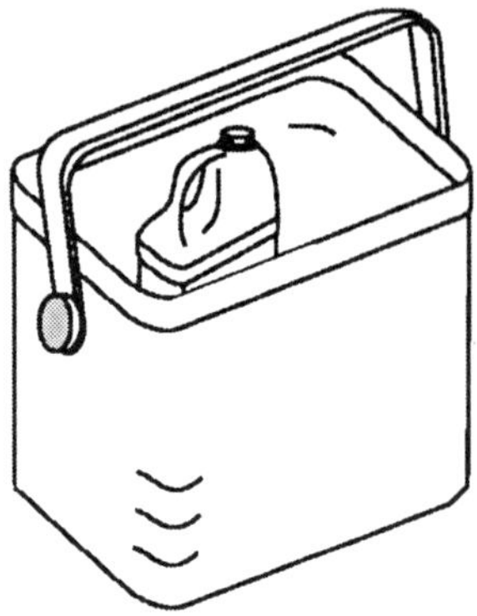

For use with a cool box and to provide iced water at the same time, fill a container and freeze. Use as you would any chemically filled cool pack.

The very large carboys, 4.5 litres and above, are valuable as they are or cut down. Use them for...

CAR OIL PANS

A large carboy with one side cut off is ideal for draining engine oil or as a tray beneath the car if you have an oil drip problem.

DRAIN COVERS

With the top and a side cut off, carboys are often large enough to make drain covers. These stop leaves and rubbish falling in and those awful smells from getting out!

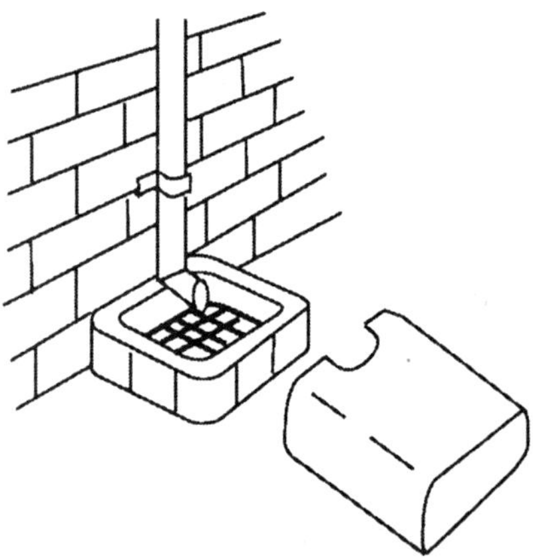

WATER CANS

Cleaned-out carboys (but only those that contained food products) make excellent water carriers for camping.

BABY EQUIPMENT STERILISING TUBS

Cut the top off to create a large, deep container – ideal for sterilising baby feeding equipment. Trim the cut-off top so it fits inside the bottom part; this makes a lid to keep the bottles submerged in the sterilising solution.

DISTILLED WATER COLLECTORS

Purified water for steam irons, car batteries, etc, is expensive – and even though it's only water, a lot of energy is used to make it. However, every time it rains distilled water falls out of the sky absolutely free – real pennies from heaven! To make a rainwater collector, choose an open site – a lawn or grass verge is ideal. Make a plastic sheet about 1 metre square from a bin liner, or a large plastic bag, and stretch it between four sticks pushed into the earth, so that the sheet is about 50cm off the ground. Pierce a few holes in the middle of the sheet and weigh down with some clean stones. Place the carboy underneath with a funnel, cut from a plastic drinks bottle, in the neck to collect the drips. Set up when it looks like rain – several minutes' downpour should fill a 4.5 litre carboy. If you haven't got a water butt, use this to collect rain water for lime-hating plants, like azaleas, as well.

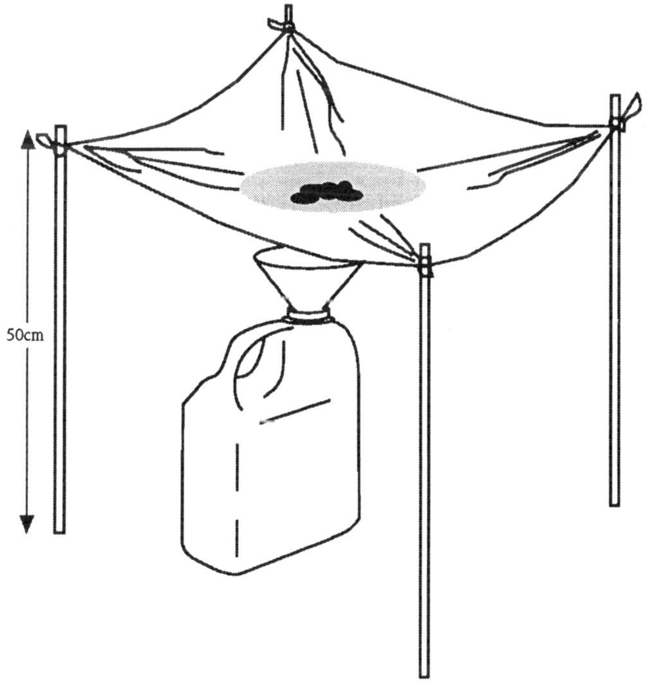

SEED TRAYS

Cut off the top of a large plastic carboy to make a good sized tray for raising all types of seedlings. Pierce drainage holes as required.

JETTY FENDERS

Large carboys, hung on piles and jetties, will help to protect small boats from scrapes and knocks when they're tied up. To make them more robust, stuff the carboys with any suitable cushioning material such as expanded polystyrene, old rags, etc.

NETS

Citrus fruits and bulk root vegetables in particular, are frequently packaged in nets varying in size from a small tube up to the size of a large sack. These are strong, light and you can see what's in them...so use these properties for...

TOY STORAGE

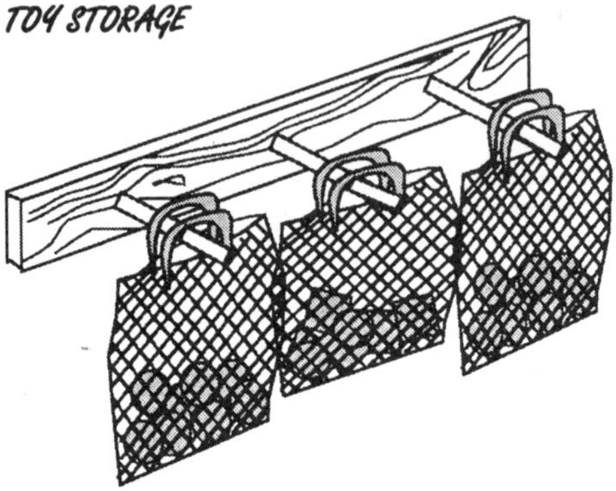

Jigsaws, duplo, balls, etc – all those annoying bits and pieces can be kept in one place in fruit nets hung up on some large hooks. Children can see what's in each bag – without emptying it out first! Nets are also very useful for organising lots of household items like dusters and polish, shoe cleaning kit, and so on.

BATH TOY HOLDERS

Plastic net bags are particularly useful for storing wet toys to drip dry in the bath – just hook the plastic handles over the tap.

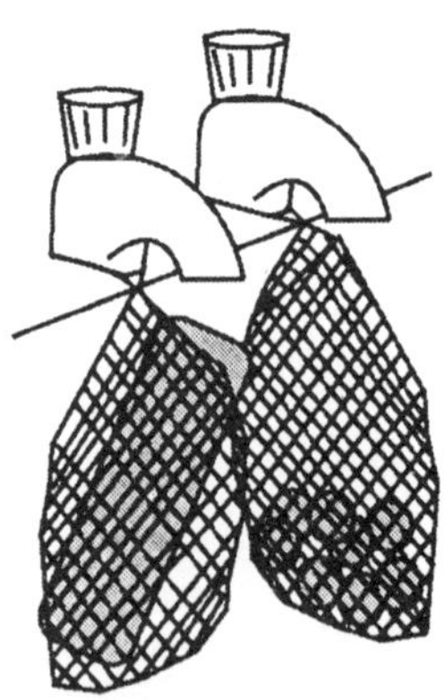

SALAD DRIERS

No need to buy a special basket or complicated rotary drier: put your lettuce into a clean fruit net and swing it briskly round (outside!). It does the job just as well.

FISHING NETS

Make a child's fishing net with a fruit net bag, a bamboo cane and a bent wire coat hanger. Uncoil the coat hanger, bend to shape and thread it through the top edge of the net. Push both ends firmly into

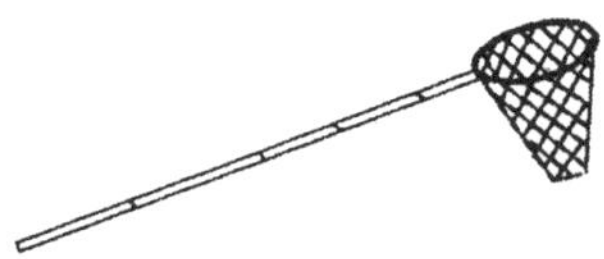

the cane. You can also use these nets for repairing broken fishing nets.

LAUNDRY BAGS

A large net threaded or sewn around a wire coat hanger makes an excellent space-saving laundry bag.

FRUIT SUPPORTS

Small nets are ideal for use as supports for melons and other heavy fruits and vegetables growing on delicate stems.

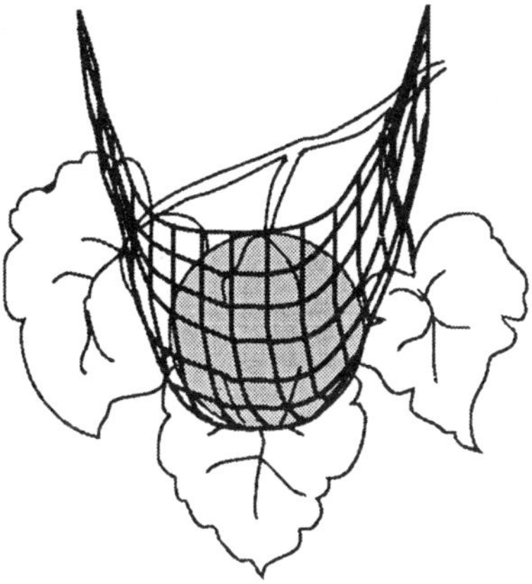

MARROW/ VEGETABLE STORAGE

Keep the fruit nets from the supermarket for hanging large vegetables for winter storage.

BLUETIT/BIRD FEEDERS

You will need a plastic net/tube, a plastic jamjar lid (peanut butter/marmite lids are ideal), and two thin sticks/twigs.
Using a hot spike or screwdriver, carefully pierce two holes straight through the opposite sides of the lid, flush with the underside. Then pierce two more holes at right angles to the first, near the bottom edge of the sides. Make sure that you have left enough space for the sticks (which will form the perches) to cross over each over. Place the pierced lid upside-down in the net. Insert the sticks through the net and holes in the lid. Fill with peanuts or birdfood, close, and hang up.

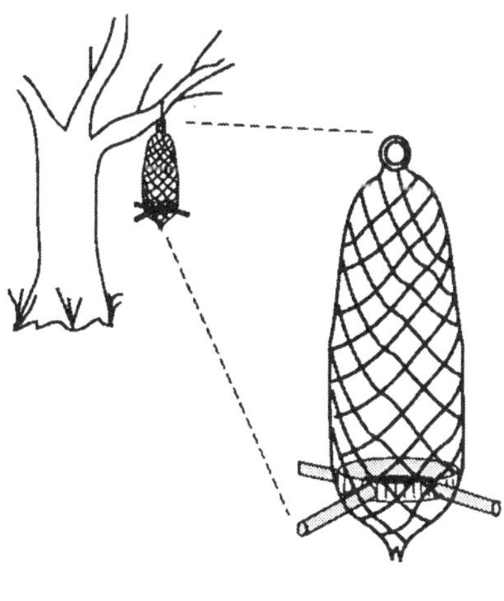

CAR AND WINDOW SCOURERS

A wet sponge wrapped inside a fine fruit net creates an excellent, no-scratch, scourer which is very effective in cleaning off insects, bird droppings and other difficult-to-remove soiling from car windscreens, paintwork and household windows. Keep one handy in your car from spring onwards, when the birds and insects are most prevalent.

When stretched over a suitable frame, such as the sides of a bottomless fruit box, the top half of a plastic bottle, etc, nets can also be used to make:

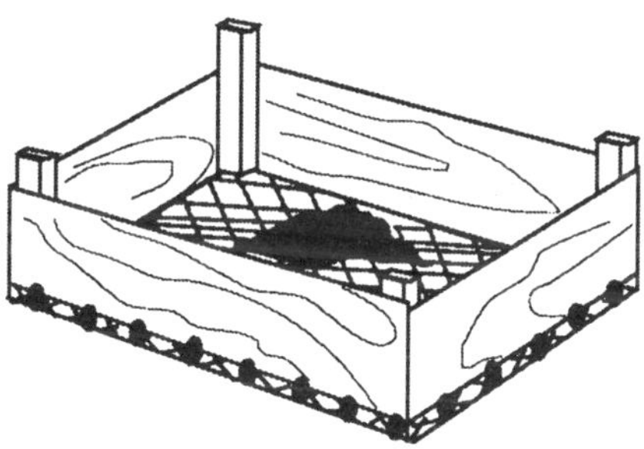

SOIL SIEVES

STRAINERS

DRYING TRAYS FOR BULBS, ETC

Use stacks of fruit boxes with net bottoms.

ALUMINIUM FOIL CONTAINERS

Take-aways, pies, ready cooked meals – many prepared foods are often packaged in foil. Most of the aluminium foil used in packaging is much thicker, more rigid and stronger than ordinary kitchen foil, so the containers are relatively robust and, with care, can be used again and again. Being metal (and aluminium at that) they also withstand, conduct and reflect heat very well, so you can make use of them as...

FREEZER CONTAINERS
Why buy special containers when you might be throwing away perfectly usable ones already?

CONTAINERS FOR LEFTOVERS
The advantage of using a foil container for this is that you can reheat the food either in the oven or by steaming straight in the container, without making another dish dirty. However, do not microwave any metal container.

STEAMERS
Place a foil container with some holes pierced in it, upside-down in the bottom of a saucepan. Put another foil dish, the right way up, on top, and you have created a very effective steamer. Longer take-away dishes are particularly useful for steaming foods which are awkward to deal with, such as asparagus and fish.

PIE DISHES
Don't throw pie dishes away; keep them for when you make your own.

PICNIC DISHES
Foil take-away dishes are just the job for picnics, and with care you can heat up food in them over a camping gas stove.

ROASTING TINS
If you just want to roast a few potatoes, onions, or a chop or two, why give yourself the bother of cleaning up a large and oily roasting dish when it is perfectly easy to use a foil container and then dispose of it afterwards?

BARBEQUE LINERS
Line the bottom of your barbeque ash pan with foil containers squashed flat. This helps to reflect the heat upwards to cook the food, keeps the pan clean, and the thicker container foil will not burn away as quickly as kitchen foil.

BIRD SCARERS
The thick foil is easily cut and bent into shapes, which can be threaded onto strings to frighten birds off.

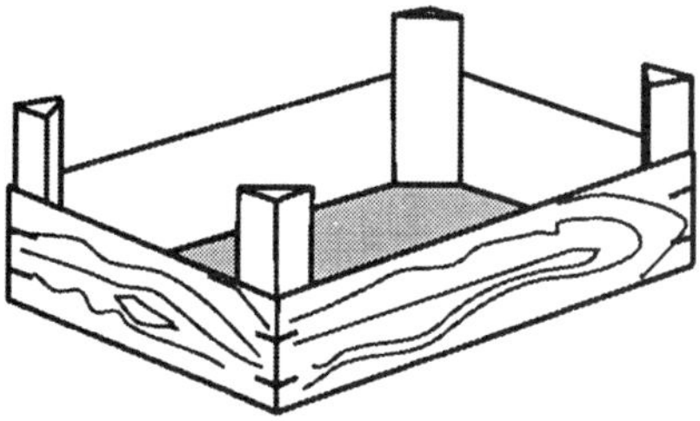

FRUIT BOXES

If you can get hold of these they are very handy indeed to have around the house. The traditional types are wooden with a hardboard or slotted wood base but increasingly many are fabricated from very thick corrugated cardboard; these are just as useful.

The cardboard boxes have lugs, which interlock with the box above when they are stacked, and no staples or sharp edges. This makes them particularly useful for...

TOY BOXES

FILES, BOOK AND PAPER STORAGE

KNITTING AND SEWING BOXES

CHEST OF DRAWERS

If you don't mind cardboard boxes stacked up around the house, they provide serviceable – and free – storage facilities for socks, underwear, etc.

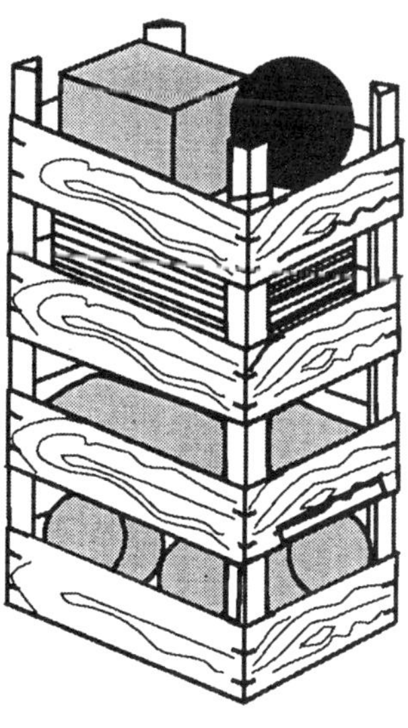

The wooden boxes are strong and moisture proof – ideal for...

RECYCLING BINS

SEED TRAYS

WINTER FRUIT AND VEGETABLE STORAGE

TOOL BOXES

VEGETABLE RACKS

PLANT POT TRAYS

And finally, if you have no further use for them, tear up the cardboard boxes, screw the pieces up and use them for...

FIRE LIGHTING

And chop up the wooden boxes for...

KINDLING

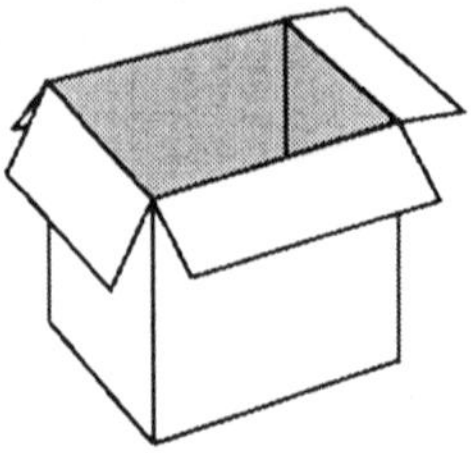

CORRUGATED CARDBOARD BOXES

This must be the archetypal reusable packaging item: we've all got stuff lying around the place stored in them. However, there are other uses for the humble cardboard box besides filling them up with junk. Corrugated cardboard has a number of properties that you can make use of in various ways. It's light and strong, and a good thermal insulator. So try using cardboard boxes for...

STORAGE

Fruit, books, clothes, paper, materials for recycling – the list is endless. Anything can be put into them (within reason) and they are often strong enough to be stacked up.

CAT/PET CARRIERS

Next time you have to transport your pet, get a good strong box big enough to take the animal. The type that are made of extra thick card are best.

Cut box flaps with locking lugs and slots, and handle slits (see bottom diagram). Exact positioning is not critical – unless you are after perfect joints – a few minutes of trial and error with a pair of scissors and a couple of boxes and you will soon get the hang of it. For the simplest handle fold up the handle slits to form handholds in the box lids. Alternatively, a rope or plastic strip loop, threaded through each handle slit and then passed through the slit on the corresponding side, will effectively close the box and also hold the top together, (see top diagram).

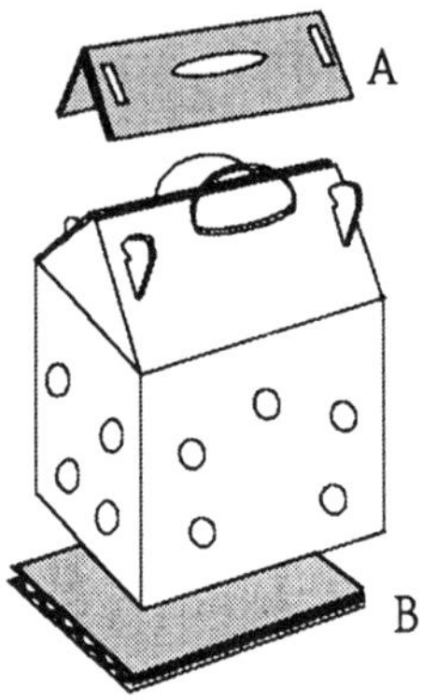

If your pet is a regular 'Houdini', make an extra roof of cardboard (A) – placing it over the lugs before closing the flaps. Similarly, if your pet is particularly heavy, put an extra cardboard bottom (B) inside the box. A real 'heavyweight' might cause the handles to tear through the lids, so you may also have to strengthen the handle area by stapling or glueing on an extra thickness of card. These pet carriers will last a long time if they are well made, they won't have cost a penny, and if your pet soils the box just throw the whole lot away and make a new one.

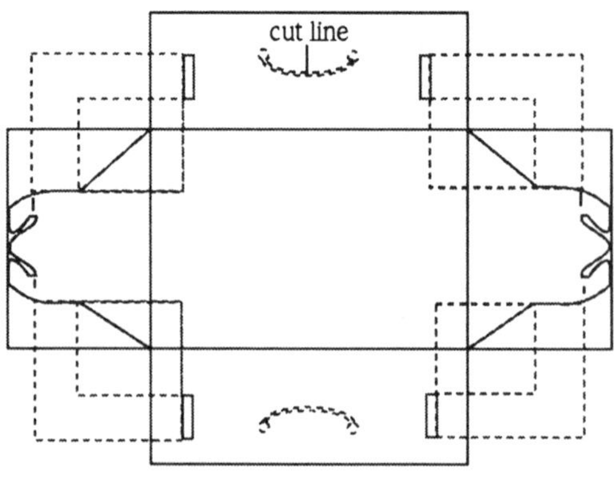

COOL BOXES

For this you will need two boxes – one made into an outer carrier (as for the pet carrier); the other to fit inside, with enough space between the two for another layer(s) of cardboard as extra insulation. (Thicken the insulation as the weather gets hotter or to keep cool for very long periods. Screwed up newspaper, or expanded polystyrene is also very effective.) If you can put items like serviettes, table-cloths, crisp packets and similar items on top of the inner box, there'll probably be enough insulation to omit the top extra cardboard layer. To contain condensation and avoid a soggy box, line the inner box with a large plastic bag, or place foods and cool packs inside in a number of plastic bags. Juice carton cool packs are just the job (see the Juice and Liquid Cartons section). Or you can, of course, use the cool packs bought from shops.

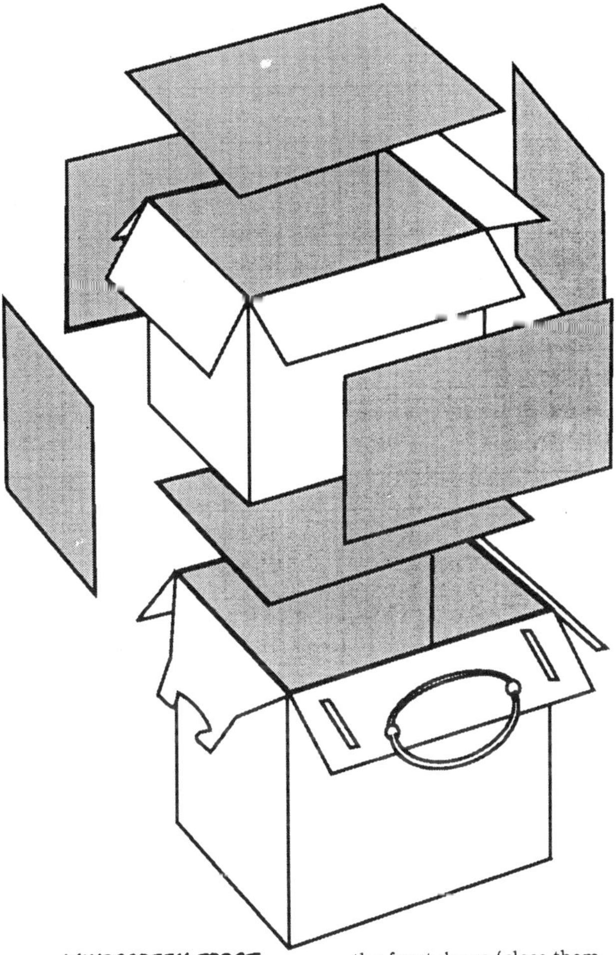

WINDSCREEN FROST COVERS

Avoid that early morning panic to scrape ice off your windscreen. Cut up a large box or stick two pieces of card together to make a cover. Hold it in place with the windscreen wipers and the front doors (close them on the cardboard). It's a good idea to make a template out of newspaper sheets taped together – keep this handy for those sudden cold snaps so you can quickly cut up card of the right size and shape.

Corrugated cardboard is soft and warm to the touch. Cut to the right size it's ideal for...

SLEEPING BAG UNDERLAYS
If you haven't got an underoll, corrugated cardboard is a good stop-gap: you can roll it up and it's disposable.

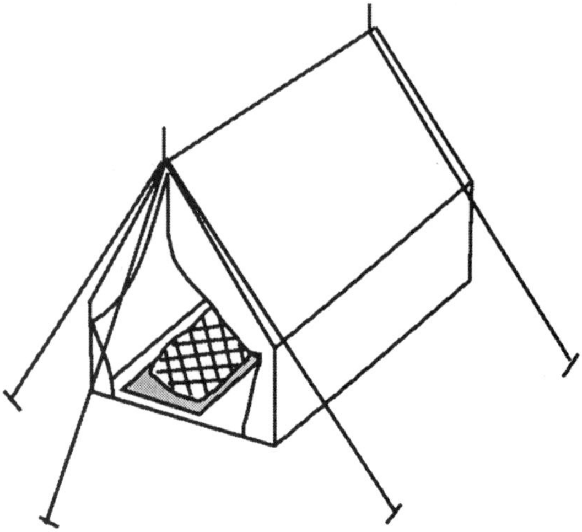

TYRE CHANGING MATS
Keep a sheet in the car for kneeling on during a tyre change.

PICNIC SEATS
Take some in a bag or cut up your cardboard cool box on arrival.

GARDENING KNEELING PADS

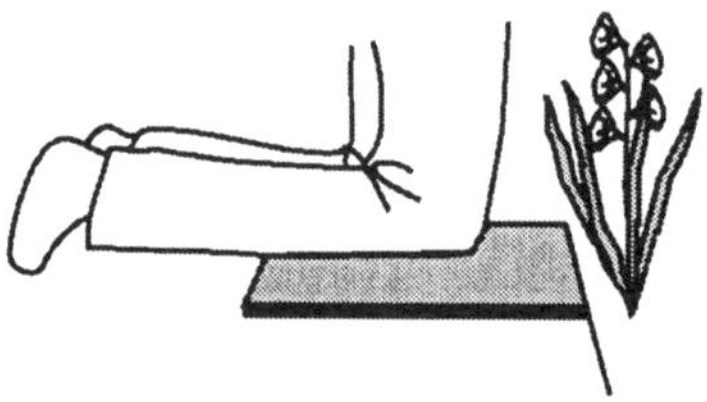

It's absorbent and makes very good disposable...

DOORMATS, CARMATS, PET FEEDING MATS

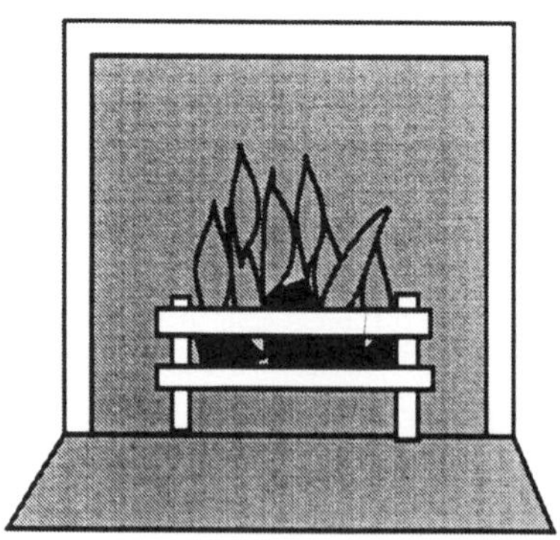

And finally it burns well. Small sheets rolled up and twisted into short sticks can be used as...

FIRELIGHTERS
You will light a fire quicker and easier with some cardboard twists added to the kindling.

PLASTIC SOFT DRINKS BOTTLES

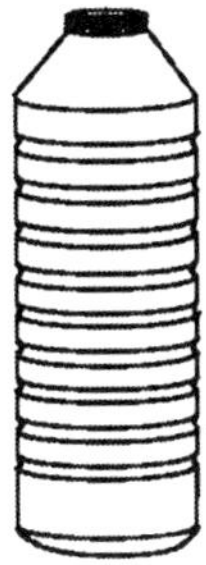

Fruit squashes and still mineral water are two common products packaged in robust plastic bottles. Like any plastic bottle they are useful as they are, and also cut up into the constituent parts. For instance...

SQUASH BOTTLING

Purpose-designed for this in the first place, these bottles are ideal for your own homemade squashes and cordials.

LIQUID FOOD STORAGE

They make excellent containers for keeping items such as stocks, sauces, or juices for preserves, in the fridge.

Like any plastic bottle with a conical top various sizes can be cut up and the tops and bottoms used for...

FLOWER POTS

Pierce drainage holes in the bottom.

FUNNELS

Make a funnel by cutting off the top of the bottle and use for pouring and siphoning liquids in the kitchen, garage or garden.

GOLF HOLE LINERS

Cut off the bottom of a bottle to fashion an ideal liner for the holes in your own pitch and putt course! Pierce a hole in the bottom for a flag and drainage.

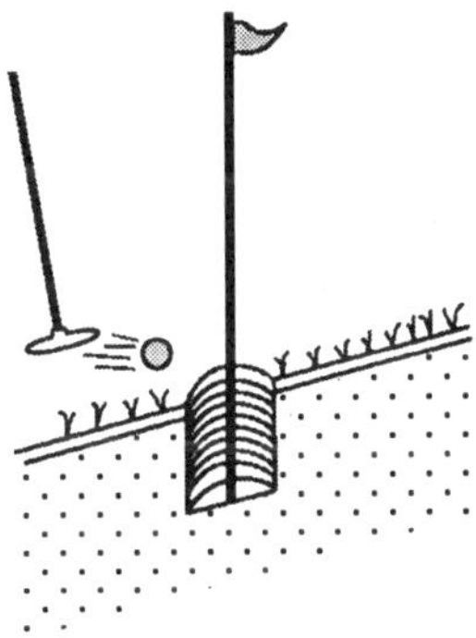

WATERING MISERS

Half bury a funnel in the ground next to plants requiring constant watering and feeding to save on time and avoid evaporation and run-off loss. The funnel directs the water to where it is needed – the roots.

ANTI-STEM ROT WATERING FUNNELS

Cut a funnel from the top of a bottle and squash to a flattish triangle. This can easily be pushed into a grow bag, large pot, or the ground, next to plants that suffer from stem rot due to watering, such as cucumbers and melons. Water and feed through the funnel.

PROPAGATION COVERS

Tops or bottoms of bottles can be placed over flower pots to protect seedlings and encourage growth. Seal tops with sellotape and polythene or a small piece of clingfilm.

You can also cut off the bottoms for use as...

ANIMAL/BIRD FEEDING DISHES

They provide useful feeding and watering dishes for cats, birds, hedgehogs...

PICNIC DISHES

Shatterproof and very functional – and they don't look too bad either!

PLANT POT HOLDERS

Simply stand the pot in the cut off bottom of the bottle to catch drainage water and stop loose compost from spoiling your window sills.

GLASS BOTTLES AND JARS

Glass presents a problem for reuse: because it is not easy to cut jars and bottles, we mostly have to find ways to reuse them as they are. Anything that involves children, of course, should be done with plastic if at all possible. Squashed plastic bottles may be unsightly but they are safe compared to broken glass.

Look out for attractive spirit bottles – many special whisky, brandy and liqueur bottles are minor works of art – as well as wine and soft drinks bottles. These types can be used for...

WINE BOTTLING

Bottle corks, incidentally, are also often reusable – provided they're not too damaged. Sterilise and insert the cork as you would any other, but seal the top of the corked bottle with melted wax.

DECANTERS

Many malt whiskies, brandies, etc, are actually packed in attractive corked decanters and the label can easily be removed. It's a great pity to throw them away when they're perfect for water or wine.

COOKING OIL BOTTLES

If you're fed up with utilitarian plastic bottles from the supermarket - decant your oil into unusual glass bottles and cork them. They will look and feel much more interesting on the shelf.

CANDLE HOLDERS

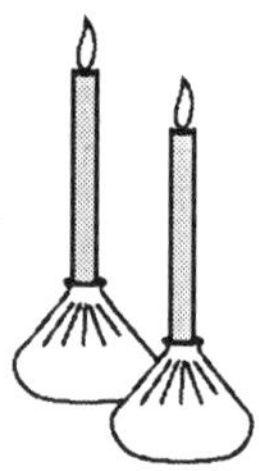

Obvious, may be, but don't forget that many bottles are more attractive than the humble wine bottle. You can even find some to colour-coordinate with your candles.

MONEY BOXES

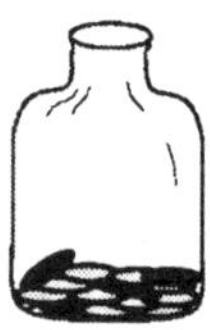

Pubs might have them on the bar but remember that children love filling them up with coins too. Save any wide-necked bottle for this.

TABLE LAMPS

The ubiquitous 'Dimple Haig' table lamp of the '60s is about to make a comeback! Or in keeping with the '90s – how about using a mineral water bottle as the base of your lamp? You can buy a bottle lightbulb fitting from many hardware and department stores.

FLOWER VASES

The necks of some bottles and jars are often wide enough but to open up the possibilities of making a wide range of unusual vases from attractive bottles you need a glass cutter.

If you're not skilled with an ordinary glass scorer, special bottle cutters are obtainable from glaziers and tool shops. Cut edges should always be smoothed off with emery paper or an oil stone before use.

Glass jars come in lots of useful shapes and sizes and colours. Most people already reuse quite a few for obvious things like...

JAMS/PRESERVES/ BOTTLING

PAINTBRUSH SOAKING

CHILDREN'S FISHING POTS

LEFTOVER FOOD CONTAINERS
Sauces, mayonnaise, tomato puree, salad dressing, etc, will store well in a jar in the fridge.

DRY FOOD STORAGE
Beans, peas, rice, dried fruit, flour, etc.

CHILDREN'S PAINT POTS

BUG COLLECTING JARS

PEN/PENCIL POTS

Less obvious uses for the right type of jar include...

CRUET SETS
Salt and pepper cruets can

easily be made out of small spice jars with plastic lids. Pierce holes in the lid with a hot spike and fill. Ideal for holidays and picnics.

NAIL AND SCREW TIDIES
To save shelf space in the workshop – or anywhere else in the house – use a collection of the same type of jar to store nails, screws, washers, fuses, and any other bits and pieces – <u>under</u> the shelf, leaving the top clear. Simply nail or screw the lids to the underside of the shelf and screw up the filled jars for storage. You'll not only save space – you can immediately see what's in the jars as well.

FLOUR/SUGAR SHAKERS
These are very easy to make from jars of a comfortable size and shape – all you

need do is pierce some small holes in the plastic lid. You will find that many jars have the same size mouth and screw thread, so if your chosen jar has a metal lid, a plastic one from another jar will often fit.

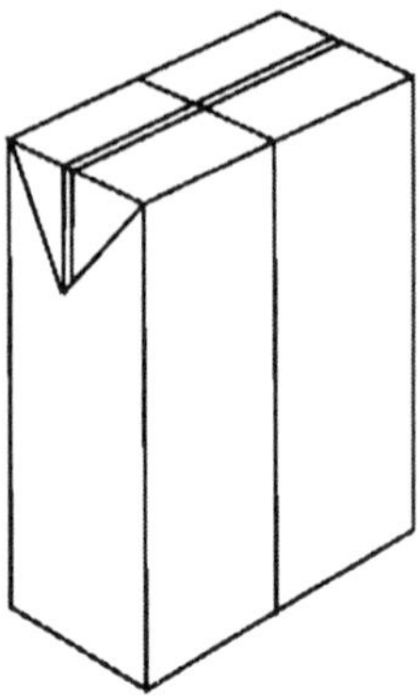

JUICE AND LIQUID CARTONS

Many people might well ask whatever can you do with these things – surely they're only made of paper and all you can do is screw them up and throw them away? However, it is surprising how useful they are. The first important factor to remember is that they are designed to contain food products and once empty can do so again. The second is that they are extremely easy to cut, staple and stick, etc: a few seconds with a pair of scissors and the carton is transformed into your creation. If you don't like 'Best Orange Juice' – or whatever else is printed on the carton – you can easily paint or cover it with some attractive material. You will find ways to use the cartons complete, cut into sheets, and cut down to various sizes. Get into the habit of cutting a small spout along the top seam, when opening the carton and this will leave you with the largest possible area with which to work.
The simplest way to reuse them is to put liquids back in...

PLANT WATERERS

You might have noticed how well cartons pour – provided the spout is cut sharply with scissors. So the next time you are about to throw one away, give it a quick rinse, fill with water and go round and water your plants: it's quick and drip free.

COOL PACKS

There is no need for special chemical-filled packs for your cool box or for keeping food packed in a box cold while travelling, etc. Ice-filled cartons will do just as well – and you'll have iced water on tap for the picnic thrown in! Fill the cartons three-quarters full, fold back the spout and stick down with sticky tape. Freeze the carton upright, overnight in the freezer. You can also fill the cartons with juice, etc, use them as cool packs, and have ice cold drinks when you arrive.

Once the cartons are washed out and dry you'll also find lots of other ways to use them complete and with the top, or a side cut off...

NESTING BOXES

Make as many of these as you like. Glue or tape the spout back down. Cut a hole in the top half (about

the size of a 50p piece for bluetits). At your chosen site, which should not be in direct sunlight, mount the carton with a couple of drawing pins inserted through the hole and a long nail just below, which also provides a perch.
For an alternative way to provide a perch, tape a couple of plastic straws to the side of the carton, projecting outwards just below the hole. For a larger box cut off one side of each of two cartons and join them together.
The cartons will keep off rain very well but pierce a couple of drainage slits in the bottom just in case.

Now all you have to do is wait and see if your local birds take a fancy to the home you've provided them with!

PAINTBRUSH SOAKERS

It's often difficult to find something to soak paint brushes in, especially long and wide ones. A throw-away 1 litre carton will take up to a10cm (4in) brush. They're OK for most common solvents – but try a little paint stripper first to test its reaction.

FLOWER POTS

All sizes of cartons are usable, either complete or cut down. They are perfectly durable, free and because they are square they take up less space on a

greenhouse bench or in a propagator.

Even with a spout already cut off, each carton cut in half will still provide you with two usable pots. Plants require drainage so pierce holes in the bottom.

PET FEEDING/ WATERING DISHES

With one side cut off cartons are perfect for

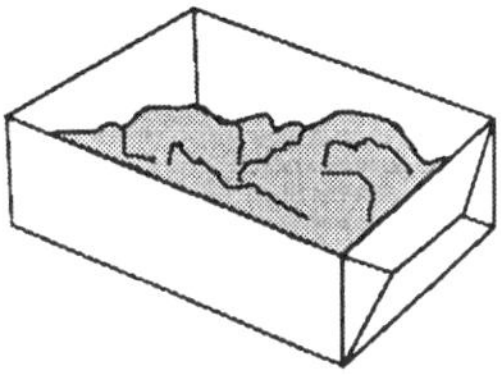

feeding and watering the dog, cat, etc, when travelling or whenever you need spare dishes.
For water dishes, tape up the cut spout, or remember to open the carton by making a cut in the top edge, and forming a spout in the side.

SANDWICH BOXES

Cartons are semi-rigid and waterproof – ideal for keeping sandwiches fresh and firm, not squashed in clingfilm or a plastic bag. Push up the top wings of the carton and cut open just under the horizontal seal. Put the sandwiches inside and close by folding down the top. There's no need to use clingfim or anything else.

Although very cheap to produce, there is a problem in recycling these cartons. They are made of multiple layers of paper, plastic and metallic materials bonded together, which are very difficult to process and separate subsequently. However, the laminated structure gives excellent strength and waterproof properties and we can make use of this. Here's some more uses which involve cutting the carton up in various ways...

CAR LITTER BINS

Cut the carton as indicated making a hole near the top of the raised top section.

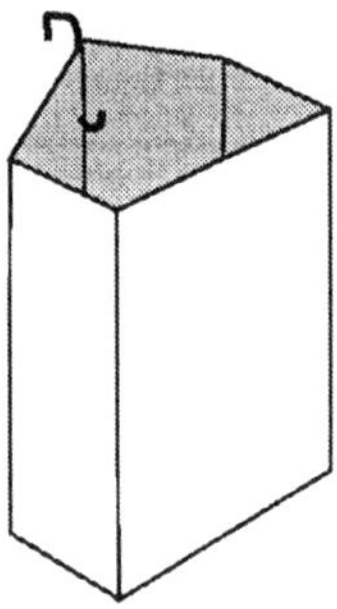

Hook over the window ledge in the car door, with a bent wire paper clip. Alternatively, use a rubber sucker hook (available from hardwear shops) to stick to the window glass.
Quick and easy to replace when full, these litter bins are ideal for all those bits and pieces of rubbish, especially if you're travelling with young children.

PLANT RING CULTURES

For tomatoes, etc, use two 1 litre cartons. Unfold all the flaps – top and bottom – and squash the carton flat. Cut just below each top and bottom seam and down the vertical seam on one side. Staple both sheets together in a ring.
This makes a good size pot which will last at least one season, and probably two. If you don't like the printing – put the metallic side outwards – both sides are sufficiently waterproof for this job.

POOP-SCOOPS

Not exactly a pleasant job – but this certainly makes cleaning up after your dog quick and painless.
Cut off the top of the carton at an angle following the guide made by the flaps on each side. Make sure the vertical seam is on the longest side – this stiffens it. Use the top part as a pusher. Once you have made your 'collection', put the whole lot in a bag (another use for that plastic bag you might have thrown away) and deposit it in an appropriate bin.
It's very easy to flatten the carton when cut and carry one in your pockets for use when out on a walk.

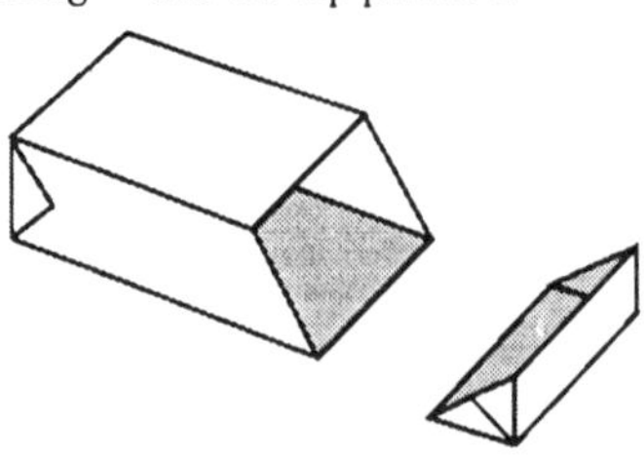

BIRD FEEDER/WATERERS

Cut carton as indicated, leaving about 1 cm of material along the bottom edge to turn over and form a lip – which helps the birds to perch. Fill with food/ water, and drawing pin to a tree, post, or stick to a window with tape.
Our record for the arrival of the first bird after siting one of these is 6 seconds! – so they certainly do work.

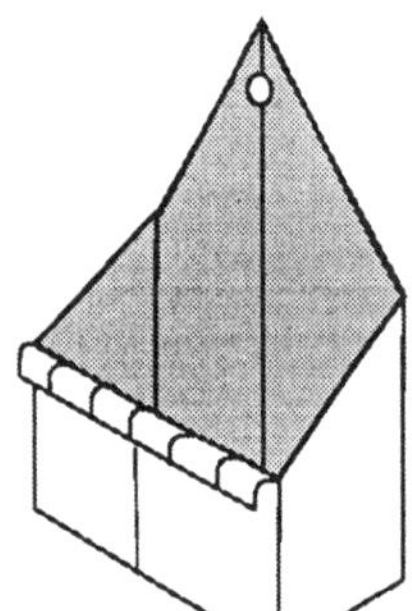

Depending on the weather, they'll last for quite a few weeks – but you can always put up new ones whenever you like.

LARGE FLOWER POTS
With a ring culture pot and a piece of cut sheet beneath it – you need never be without a large pot. These are useful for growing on large plants which don't like having their roots disturbed by transplanting – just dig the hole, remove the bottom and peel off the pot.

DISH COVERS
Save on clingfilm or dirtying your plates and saucers! Cut sheets are ideal for covering food dishes in the fridge. They are quite firm so you can also stack light dishes on top of one another.

BIRD SCARERS
The alternating flashing and turning of the reflective metallic inner surface will help to deter birds. Cut the sheet into different shapes and suspend from threads over your vulnerable, growing plants. You can make them stronger, and reflective on both sides, by glueing two sheets together back to back. Weight with Blu-Tak or plasticine to steady if necessary in a strong wind.

BARBEQUE LIGHTS
Take advantage of the reflective inner surface to make attractive lanterns for your summer barbecues. Cut the carton at a steep angle and put a night light inside, so that the flame is well away from the inner film surface. Fix up with a drawing pin, and light.

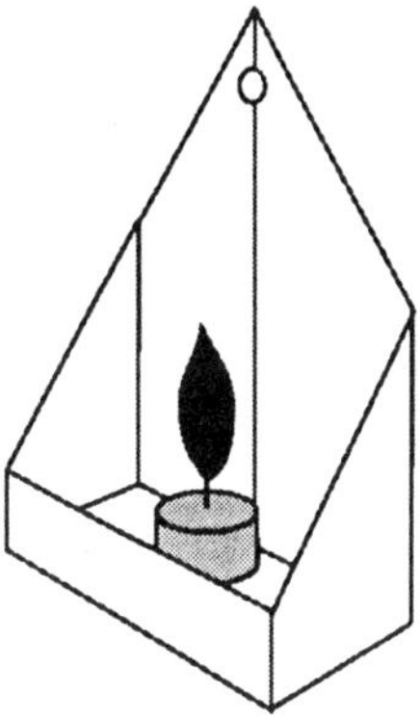

Children will also love making...

PENCIL HOLDERS

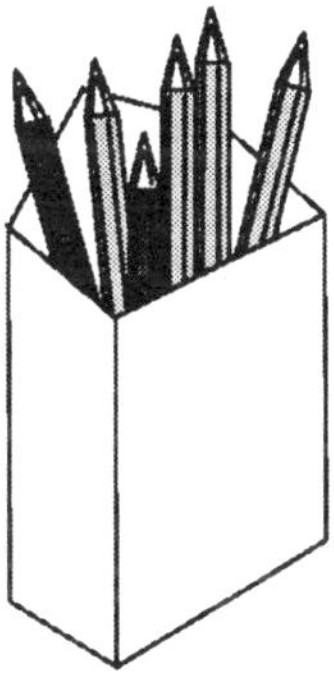

DESK TIDIES

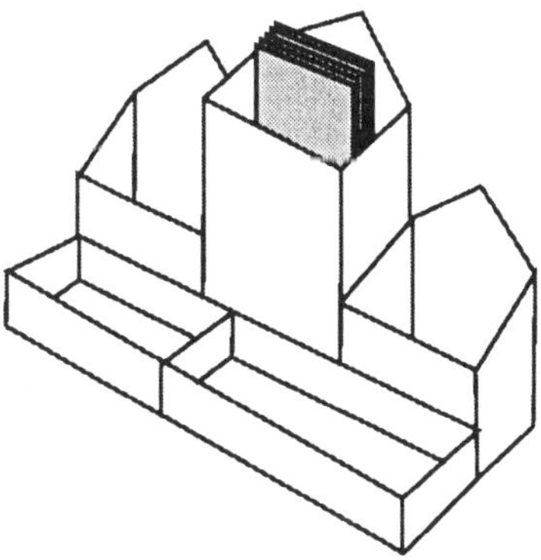

PAPER/ ENVELOPE HOLDERS
Pin one by the phone.

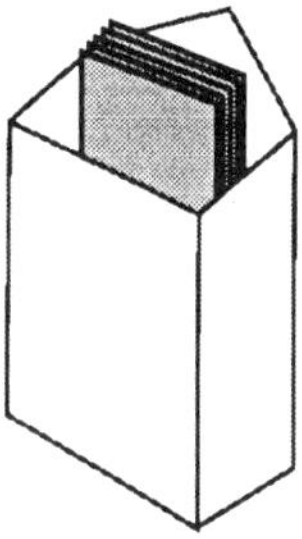

You can also use the cartons with the top cut off for...

FOOD LEFTOVER STORAGE
In the fridge.

DIY FILLER MIXING BOWLS
You'll never have to clean out a mixing bowl again!

COLLECTING BOXES
Great for storing bits and pieces like nails, screws and milk bottle tops – and they stack easily on a shelf because they are square sided.

And finally, if you're feeling ambitious...
You can get into cartons in a big way: it's even possible to make a completely disposable picnic set from them!

SPOONS
Cut strips of sheet about 5cm wide, bend into a scoop shape as shown and use as spoons.

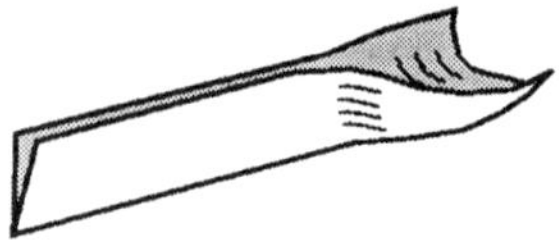

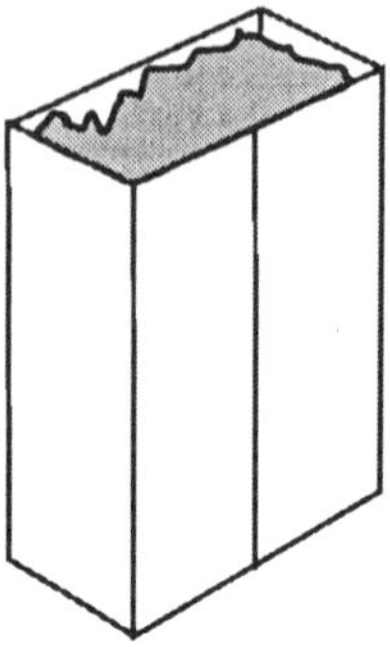

FOOD HOLDERS
Cut the top seam off and put your sandwiches/ food in the box. Fold over the top again to seal up. If the food is 'loose' or slightly too 'liquid', be sure to keep the carton upright.

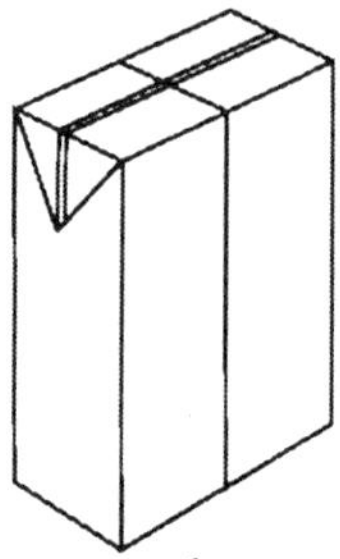

PLATES AND BOWLS
Cut the sides off to make serviceable and hygenic plates and bowls.

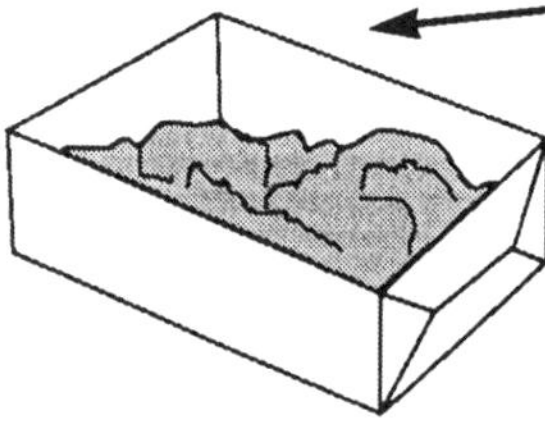

PLATTERS
Use cut up cartons as plates and stands for sandwiches, cakes, bread, etc.

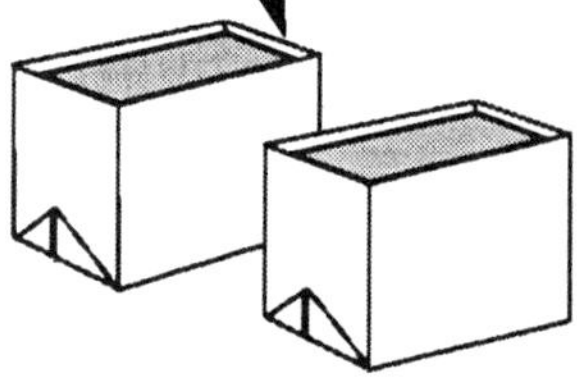

CUPS AND DISHES
Cut off the bottom half for drinking cups and dishes – hot tea and coffee is OK – but not boiling water.

You can't make a knife and fork yet from them – but we are working on it!
Put the whole lot in a cardboard box carrier (see the section on Corrugated Cardboard Boxes) and include a large paper/plastic sack to cut and use as a tablecloth. When you arrive cut up the box for seats and when you've finished wrap the whole lot in the bag. Not the most elegant way to eat alfresco – but it's so simple, and it doesn't cost you a penny...not to mention saving on the washing up!

YOGURT AND DESSERT POTS

Over the last few years there has been a tremendous growth in the amount of cream, yogurts, desserts, etc, packed in plastic pots. Advances in technology have achieved significant savings in the energy and materials required to make them and yogurt pots are now usually paper-thin – too thin for most practical uses. However, there is always a demand from schools for all sorts of pots for craft usage and we can reuse them for...

FLOWER POTS

An obvious use: virtually all the sizes and shapes are suitable for potting up seedlings or smaller plants.

GARDEN CANE COVERS

Each year there are thousands of 'eye' accidents in the garden. To avoid the risk of injury to eyes and face from not 'seeing' the cane when you bend down to tend your plants, put a pot on each cane/plant stick.

DISPOSABLE CUPS

Not as elegant or ergonomic as they might be, but perfectly usable. The pots are made of the same material as plastic cups. Disposable and safe, unlike a jamjar, there is no risk of broken glass.

PAINT AND WATER POTS

Ideal for mixing-up children's powder paints and holding water for watercolour painting.

PICNIC DESSERT POTS

It's easy to refill these pots with homemade desserts and seal with clingfilm for disposable picnic dishes. Keep a bag full of washed out pots for when you need them.

TOY INTERCOMS

Thread and knot a piece of string through a hole in the bottom of two pots. Tell the children to stretch it tightly all the time and speak to each other through them. They'll have great fun.

PEN/PENCIL HOLDERS

FIZZY DRINKS BOTTLES

These are one of the most useful of all packaging containers – there are so many things you can do with them. Here are some ideas especially for the plant enthusiast or gardener...

FLOWER ARRANGING ROSES

Bottle tops can help support long/heavy stems and conserve moisture at the same time. Pierce holes with a hot wire or screwdriver over the surface and use placed over 'Oasis' or other absorbent plant material.

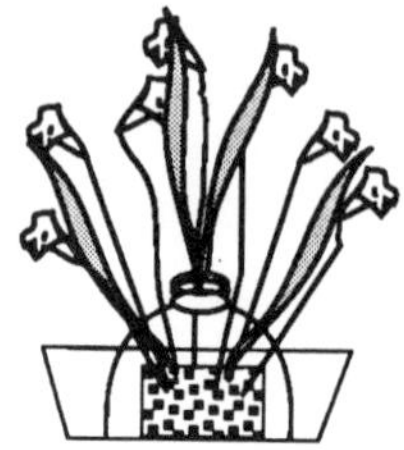

GLAZING

The material bottles are made from is very strong and is excellent for temporary glazing and greenhouse glass repairs. Fix with tape, or under existing clips.

PLANT PROTECTION/PROPAGATION

Cut off the bottom part of the container to the height required. Dome or star shaped bottoms are equally effective.

PLANT POT STANDS

CUTTINGS TRAYS

Cover with cut bottom part of bottle or a plastic bag for propagating.

PROPAGATION COVERS

Seal top with clingfilm or sellotape. Use over pots or in the garden for individual plants.

WATERING MISERS

This is a labour and water saving device that makes sure that valuable water goes direct to the roots with the minimum of run-off or evaporation loss – very useful in these days of water shortage and hosepipe bans. Just bury the top in the soil at an angle pointing towards the roots.

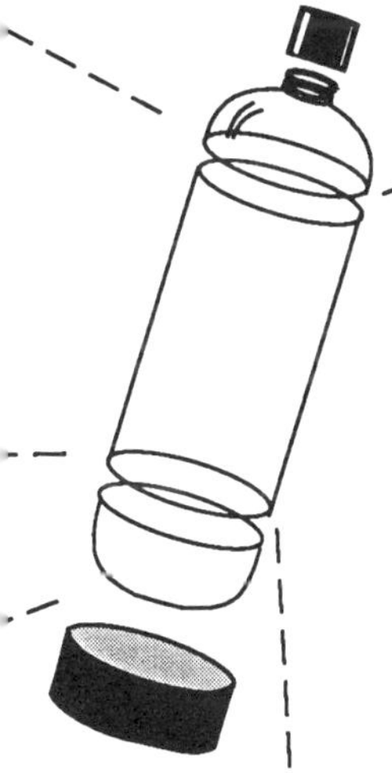

TOMATO RING CULTURE

Mid-sections from 2 litre bottles stapled together make a perfect, virtually 9in (23cm), standard pot.

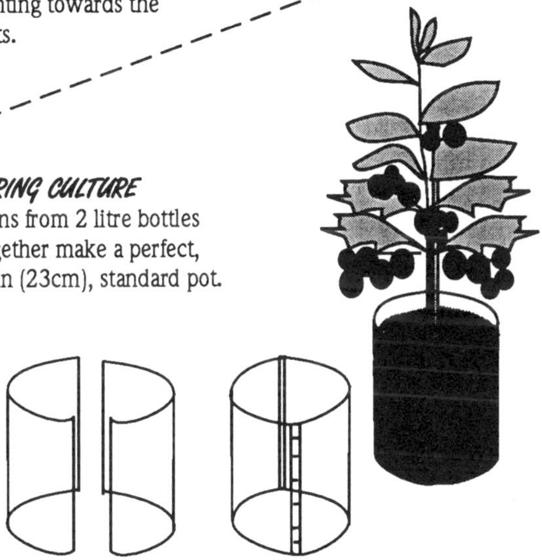

CLOCHES

Staple sheets together to form a longer/larger cloche, and hold down with bent wire coat hangers if necessary. You can also cut bottles lengthwise to form mini-seedling cloches.

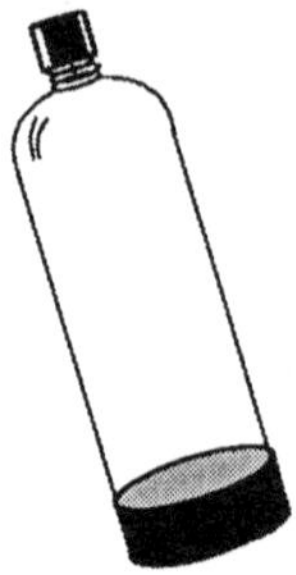

Apart from the amazing number of uses that can be found for these bottles, the great thing about them is that they're so easy to work with. They can be cut with scissors or a sharp knife. You can pin, staple, glue, crease and tape them and holes are instantly pierced with a hot metal spike, screwdriver or the like – if you do this, however, be sure to ventilate the room and remember that melted plastic can cause very bad burns – so take care.

To make these clever everyday objects required a lot of research and technology, so it is a great waste not to make further use of them. Here's a selection of other things you can do...

WITH THE WHOLE BOTTLE...

HOME BREWING

Fizzy drinks bottles are ideal for any home brewing or carbonated drinks –they are designed for them! Even if your bottles of elderflower champagne do explode there won't be any flying glass!

MONEY BOXES

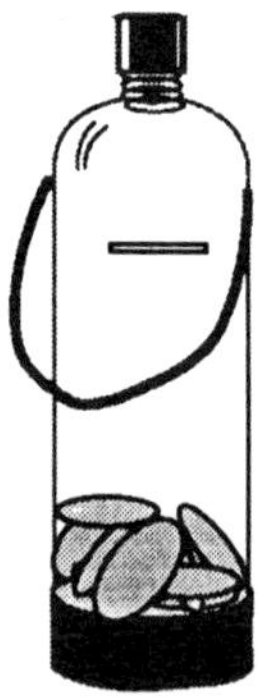

Children can easily make these and they look great filled up with coins. Charities can add a string handle, seal and put on a label, and use as a no-cost collection box. Cut a slot with a sharp knife or scissors in any appropriate bottle.

HOT WATER BOTTLES

For guests or for travelling they make perfectly good hot water bottles – but don't put boiling water straight into them. Let the water cool for several minutes after boiling or fill from the hot tap and then wrap with a towel or jumper. The bottle will probably warp – but it doesn't leak – unless you sit on it...

TEMPORARY BOAT FENDERS

They burst if you hit them very hard, or with something sharp, but then they don't cost anything do they? Pressurise by adding a couple of teaspoons of stomach antacid powder to the bottle, pour in a little water and screw on the cap quickly to capture the fizz.

CYCLISTS' WATER BOTTLES

Use a convenient size of bottle and pierce a hole through the cap to take a straw if required. To seal the straw, push through quickly while the plastic is still melted.

To make a clip, bend a wire coat hanger as shown. (You'll need a pair of pliers for this, and something to act as formers to bend the wire around –about the rough diameter of the frame and for the bottle.) Tape to the frame if necessary.

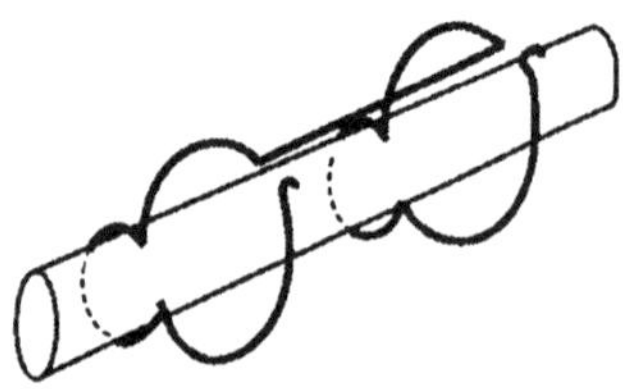

BIRD TABLES

Birds are not too fussy about the packaging that their food comes in! Use wire/string through or around the cap as a hanger. Cut panels out of the bottle sides and turn over the bottom edge to form a lip which helps the birds to perch. Similarly pierce holes and insert straws/sticks through the bottom as shown (seal holes with glue if using for water – or insert a dish cut from the bottom of another bottle). Adjust the size of cut panels to keep out larger birds if you wish, and then hang and have fun seeing if the squirrels can crack it!

FISHERMAN'S FLOATS

The collar around the neck of most bottles makes it very easy to secure a line to them. Use for nets and lines or tied in bundles for buoys. Pressurise if required as for boat fenders above.

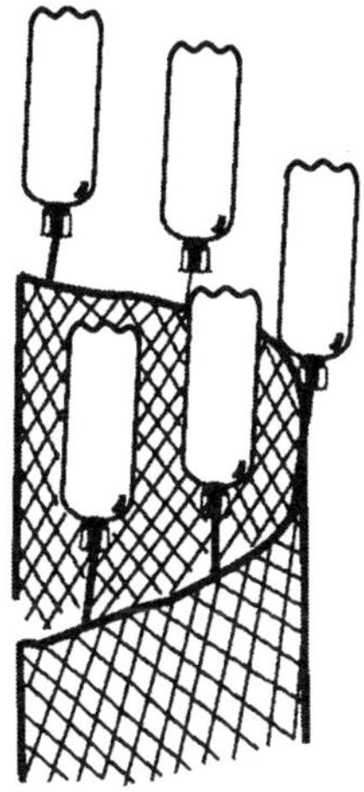

WITH CUT DOWN BOTTLES...

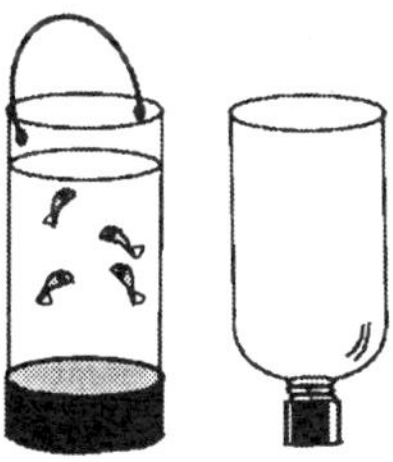

PETROL FUNNELS

Keep one in the car with the spare petrol can and make sure that your expensive petrol goes straight into the tank – not all over the road. Cut at an angle as indicated.

KIDS' FISHING POTS

Extemely quick and easy to make. Pierce two holes around the rim and use string or garden twine for handles. Children love pond dipping or collecting tadpoles in them and, unlike a jamjar, there is no risk whatever of cuts from broken glass.

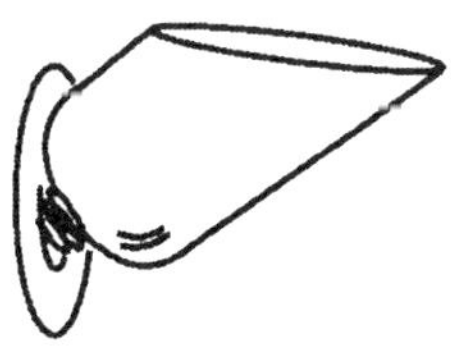

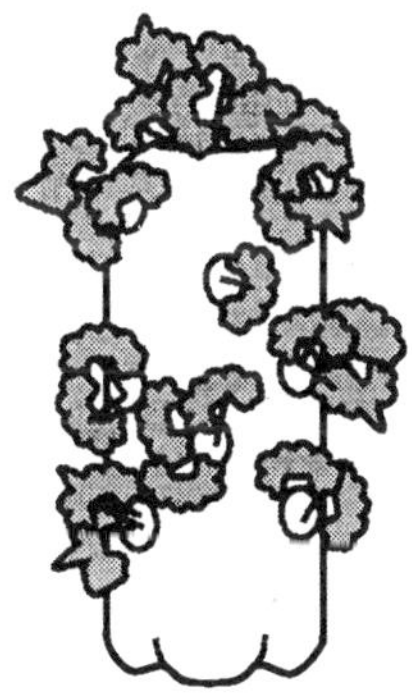

PARSLEY/HERB POTS

Have as many potted herbs on the kitchen window sill as you like. These are free and very simple to make. Cut the top and planting holes in the sides as indicated. Water through the top and pierce drainage holes in the bottom. Alternatively place some broken crockery pieces in the bottom to act as a sump for excess water.

FLOWER VASES

Just the job whenever you're stuck for a vase for

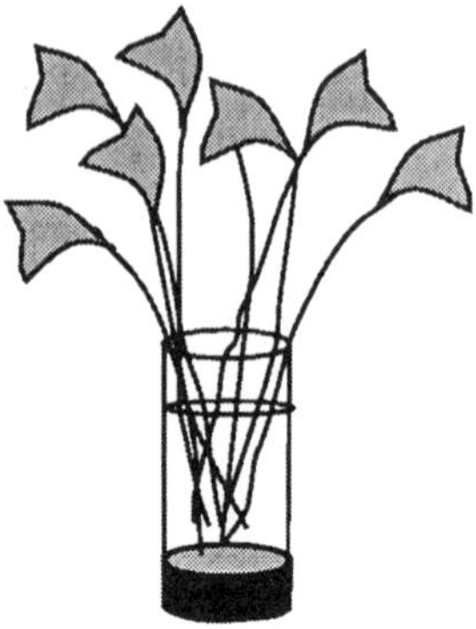

tall stems, or simply have too many flowers. Roses and daffodils look pretty in these, especially the green bottles.

RADIATOR HUMIDIFIERS

Radiator humidifiers are only required temporarily, to counter the unpleasant drying effects of central heating, so why buy something, when these come free? Cut off the top and push through a bent wire coat hanger as

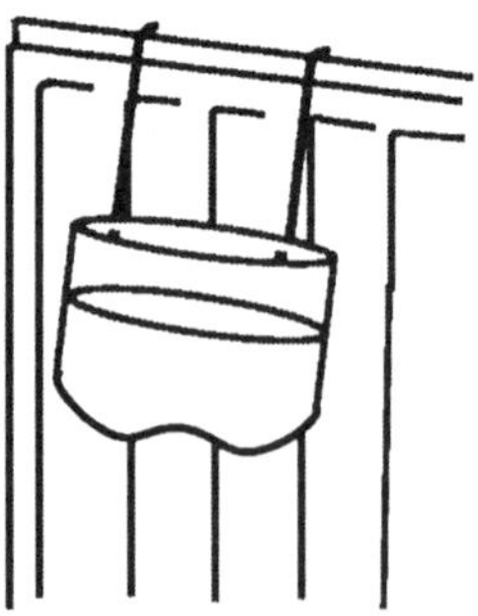

indicated to hook over the radiator. At the end of winter you can feel quite relaxed about throwing the whole lot away.

RAIN GAUGES

Here's one for the adventurous and the keen gardener. Two bottles are required, one that fits inside the other. Cut the top off both and stand the smaller inside the larger as indicated. Push the larger top, upside-down, into its bottom half and then spend an informative half an hour in your local library

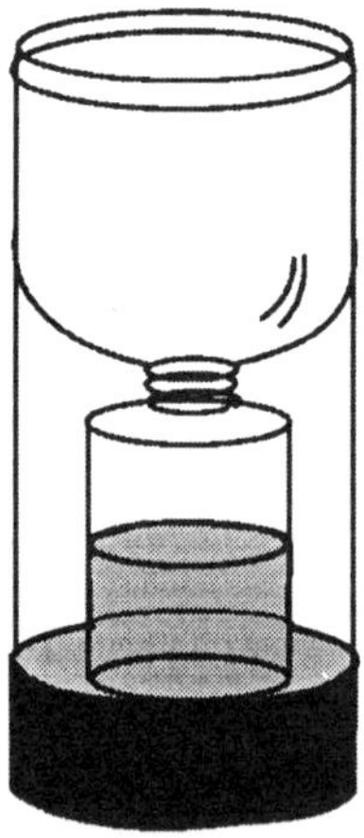

working out how to calibrate the gauge and the best place to site it. Screw or nail through the base to a post or piece of wood, or weight the large bottle with stones to stop the gauge blowing over.

ROOT CONSTRAINERS

Useful for mint and managing your herb garden, or to stop any other plant

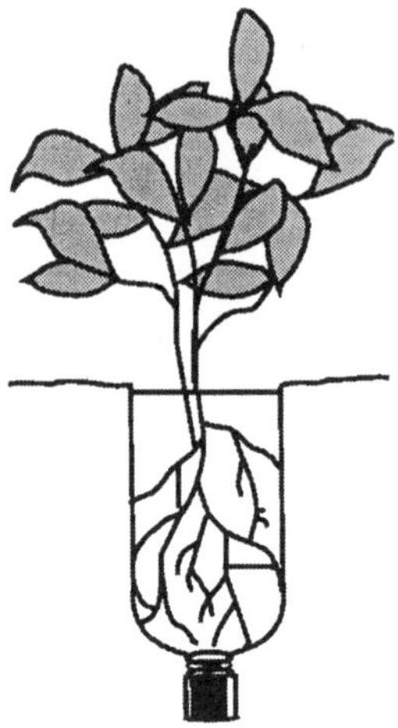

taking over the garden. Using the appropriate size of bottle, bury it upside-down and remember to water into the bottle especially in dry weather. You can also try leaving the cap off to encourage the plant to send down tap roots for water which will not tend to spread as much as the lateral roots.

KITCHEN FUNNELS

The top halves of bottles are useful for pouring or filtering (with filter paper/medium) almost anything except boiling or very hot liquids. For a longer neck, tape on a tube rolled from plastic sheet cut from the sides of the bottle.

NON-SPILLABLE PAINT POTS

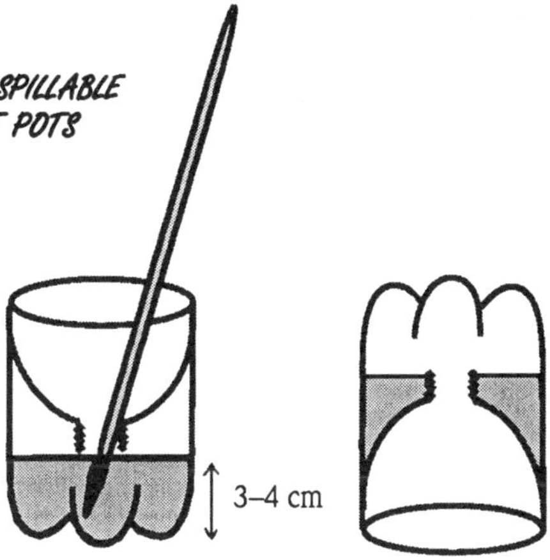

This is an amazing device – turn it upside-down or knock it over and the paint or water will not come out. Cut off the top of a bottle, just below the point where the curved top meets the vertical side. Shorten the bottom half so that there will be a 3-4 cm gap between the base of the bottle and the top of the neck, when the top part is pushed upside-down into its bottom half. Gently push in for a press fit.

If the contact between the two halves is loose, or if it kinks, seal with tape.

Fill with paint, glue, water, etc, to just below the neck and have a lot of fun showing everybody that it doesn't spill.

This is an essential reuse of packaging for every parent of young children or primary school teacher in the land!

MILK BOTTLE COVERS

Cut off the bottom of a bottle to leave you with an ideal cover to keep the birds off your milk. Pierce some holes in the top and bottom for ventilation and paint with white emulsion – which will help to keep the milk cool in summer and delay freezing in winter.

GOLDFISH BOWLS

Next time your kids win some fish at the fair, a large 3 litre bottle with the top cut off is just the job until you get around to buying a proper bowl!

WITH THE MIDDLE BIT...

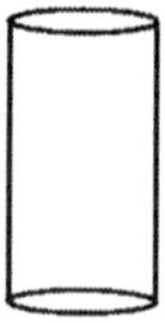

These provide a ready supply of material which is extremely strong and very easy to cut. Useful for modelling, making tubes, or any time you need to use bits of plastic sheet. Here are a few more ideas...

HEAD LAMP PROTECTORS

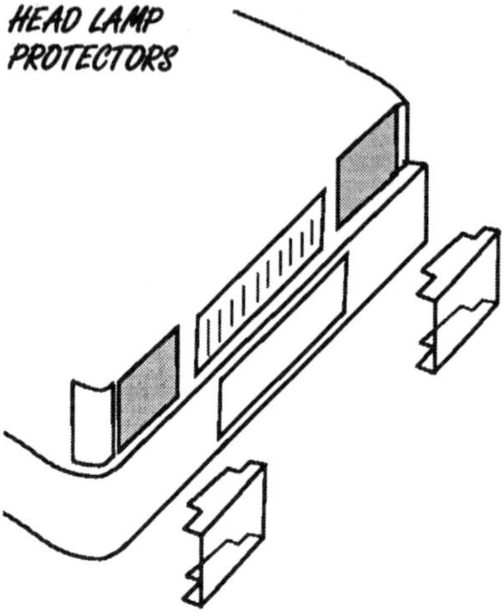

Open the bonnet and by trial and error use a sheet of paper to draw up a template. Most headlamp units are held in by a number of screws and you can use these for gripping. Alternatively, stick the protectors down with tape.

Most car accessory suppliers and garages sell these, but it's easy to make your own by cutting and bending the sheet. Not as robust as the bought ones which are thicker, but they certainly give added protection against chips and damage. If you need to paint your headlamps yellow or fit beam masks for going abroad you can also do this with a spare kit of protectors – which saves having to clean up the headlamps when you come back.

VACUUM HOSE EXTENSIONS/TOOLS

It costs nothing to make vacuum extensions for awkward places. Roll up the sheet and stick with sellotape to form tubes which will fit over the long tool of your vacuum cleaner hose. Join several tubes

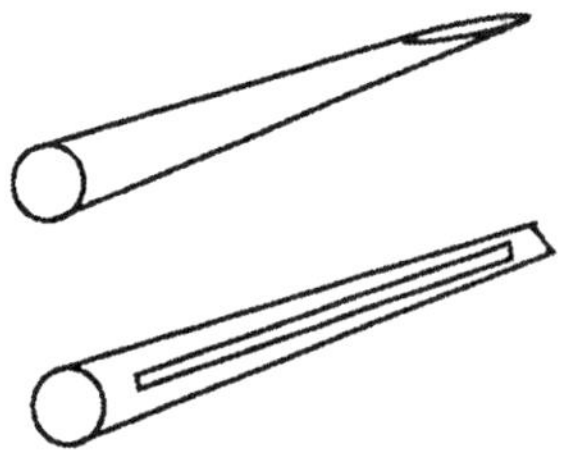

together if required. Squash the end and cut at an angle for behind radiators, inside central heating boilers and so on, or seal the end and cut a long slot for cleaning the floor under cookers and fridges.

STENCILS

The bottle plastic provides a perfect free substitute for expensive acetate stencil sheet. First roll it up tightly in the opposite direction to lessen the curl. Then cut with a sharp knife, or a scalpel for intricate designs.

WITH THE TOPS AND BOTTOMS...

PASTRY/BISCUIT CUTTERS

Cut like this... or this... this... or this.

Also try different sizes of bottle. You may need to use a small saw to cut the thicker parts of the tops and bottoms.

SINK AND LOO PLUNGERS

Leave the cap on and cut the top off to roughly the size of a plunger, with a very straight rim. Block the

overflow with a rag, fill the sink and pump the top vigorously up and down over the plughole as you would a rubber plunger – it will remove all but the most stubborn blockages. As the top is semi-rigid, it can be used for unblocking toilets too. Use the biggest bottle that will fit into the bottom of the toilet bowl, and, if preferred, push and seal a stick into the neck.

PLANT POT SAUCERS/HUMIDIFIERS

Flower pots will stand on the ridges of a star-shaped bottom, holding the pot clear of drainage water. For extra humidifying effect, stand the pot on gravel or small pebbles, and keep

topped up with water, ensuring the pot bottom is clear of the water level.

FLOWER-HEAD DISHES

Single blooms or small groups of flowers look very pretty floated on water in these at the dinner table.

The star-shaped bottoms also provide a ready supply of dishes which can be used for things like...

JELLY MOULDS

SOAP DISHES

POT-POURRI DISHES

ARTISTS'/CHILDREN'S PAINT PALLETS

DESK TIDIES

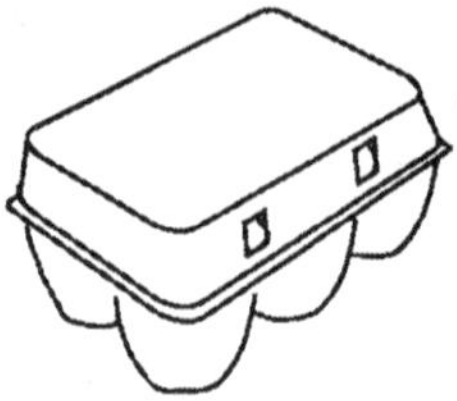

EGG BOXES AND TRAYS

Egg boxes are one of the few containers that can be returned for refilling – at least by local suppliers. However, if you can't find anybody who wants to put more eggs back into them don't despair! There are lots of ways to reuse them but for food and drink purposes be sure to thoroughly clean and rinse the plastic ones first. Although it's a slight risk, some boxes may be contaminated with micro-organisms from the eggs.

The plastic varieties can be put to use as...

LOLLIPOP MOULDS

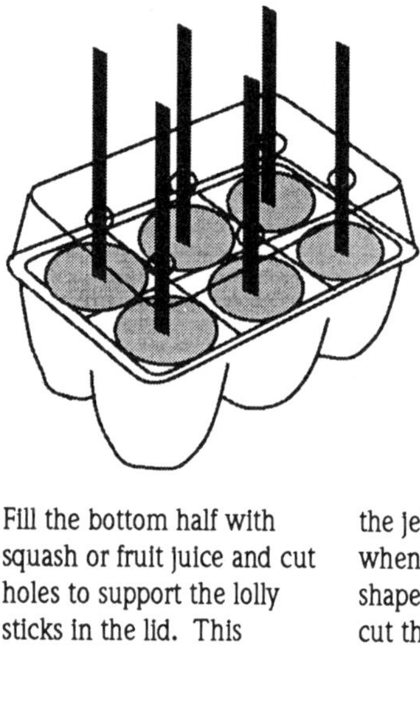

Fill the bottom half with squash or fruit juice and cut holes to support the lolly sticks in the lid. This makes small lollies which will not ruin a child's appetite before meals!

ICE TRAYS

Fill the bottom half of a plastic egg box with water and freeze. Break up the ice when frozen and store in the freezer.

JELLY MOULDS

If you don't have a mould, fill the bottom half of a plastic egg tray with the jelly solution and tip out when set for an interesting shaped jelly. You can also cut the jelly into strips to make a snake, dragon or caterpillar jelly, or divide it into individually decorated portions.

Use the papier mâché types for...

PET BEDDING

A box with egg trays, a layer of cardboard on top and a blanket or rug, makes a well insulated and comfortable bed for dogs and cats.

FIRELIGHTERS

Screwed up papier mâché egg boxes and trays have more fuel value and allow for better air circulation than newspaper, and are much more effective for fire lighting.

FLOWER AND HERB DRYING TRAYS

The trays provide ideal support, absorbency and air circulation for drying herbs and flowers. They make it easy to move your delicate specimens if they get in the way.

WINTER FRUIT STORAGE

Pack apples, pears, etc, in cardboard or wooden boxes between layers of egg trays. The egg trays will separate and cushion the fruit and allow air to circulate, which is essential for keeping the fruit in good condition.

Any type – and particularly the larger papier mâché trays with a clear plastic lid that supermarket chains commonly put eggs in – also make very serviceable...

SEEDBOXES AND TRAYS

Fill any box or tray with the appropriate compost or growing medium to provide a quick and free seed tray – particularly useful if you don't need to fill up a full-sized traditional seed tray. Egg boxes provide enough depth of compost for most plants and wet papier mâché will usually stay together long enough to raise seedlings big enough for potting on.

SEEDLING PROPAGATORS

You can make a very simple propagator from a papier mâché tray and two plastic lids. Cut a little off the edges of the tray so that it will fit neatly inside the lower upturned lid. Fill the tray with compost and seeds and place the other lid on top. Follow seed supplier's instructions regarding light or dark conditions. An appropriate heat source may be necessary, but you will find that one of these trays placed on a south-facing window sill will raise many seedlings very effectively.

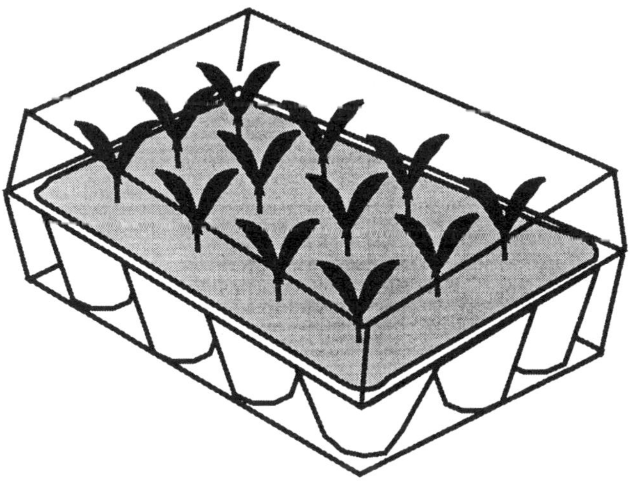

PLASTIC BUCKETS

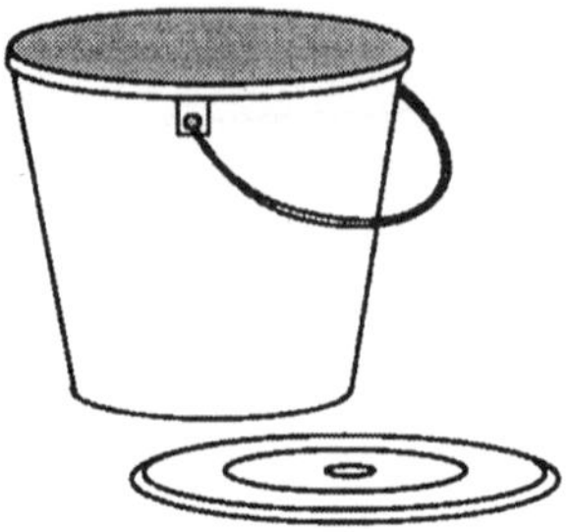

Washing powders, ice cream, DIY fillers and finishes are frequently packaged in buckets, partly because of the bulk involved and partly with the idea of making the product more attractive by providing a free bucket. So the idea of reusing the packaging has already been introduced when you buy it, but many people still just throw these handy containers away. Consumer packaging buckets come in a wide range of sizes up to about the size of a domestic house bucket and you will find uses for all of them with or without the lid. They can be used as a source of plastic for fashioning simple items but they are probably most valuable reused as buckets. Possibilities include...

PAINT KETTLES

Not quite as good in use as a vertical sided kettle, made from a large tin can, but almost as good for making painting easier and cleaner.

HOUSEHOLD BUCKETS

Several large buckets around the house and garden will always come in useful so don't throw away any of the right size.

BEACH AND SANDPIT BUCKETS

FLOWER POTS

TOY STORAGE

A lidded bucket is ideal for storing and stacking those bits and pieces that get everywhere – lego, toy animals, marbles, etc.

TODDLER STEP UPS

If you have small children a large, wide and fairly steep-sided bucket makes a stable and free step-up platform for teeth-cleaning, hand-washing, etc. Keep one in the bathroom.

There are also ways to re-use buckets cut down to make a variety of dishes and bowls...

BULB GROWING BOWLS

PET FEEDING/ WATERING DISHES

PLANT POT COASTERS

CARD PACKETS AND CARTONS

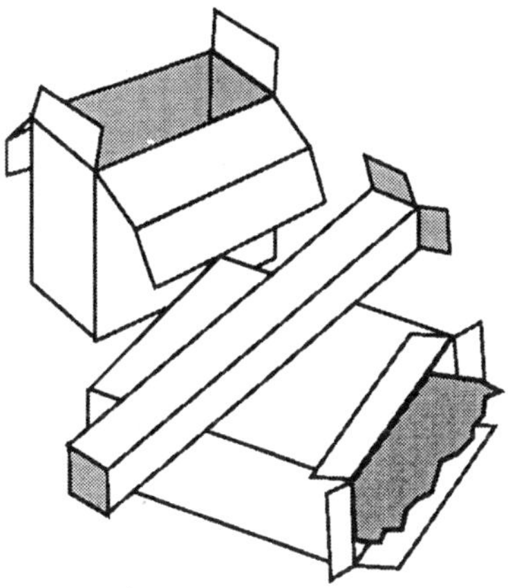

Toothpaste cartons, cereal packets, washing powder boxes – the list is endless. There are literally hundreds of products which are packaged in this way. We've used them for toy and model-making for years, but look out for boxes especially suitable for...

WRAPPING PRESENTS

Cover with attractive paper for an expensive-looking present box, free and just as good as one from the shops.

You will also save a lot of money and time by making a collection of pieces of card with attractive pictures/designs on them for use as...

POSTCARDS

CALENDAR BACKS

GREETINGS CARDS

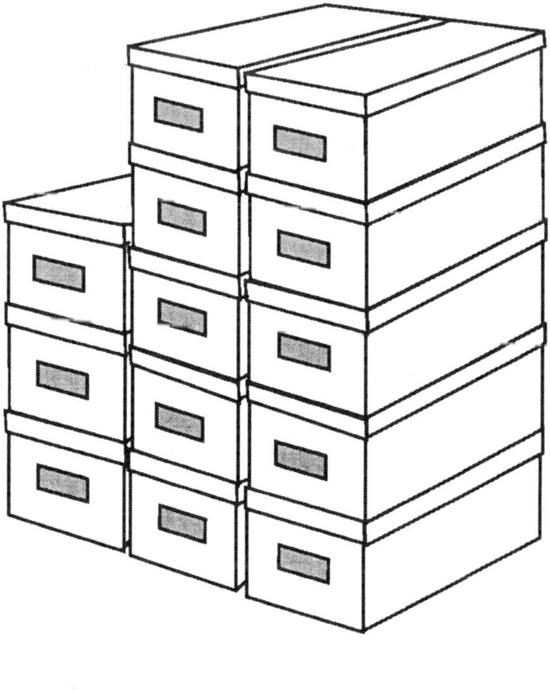

PACKED LUNCH BOXES

Stop sandwiches and crisps from getting squashed by putting them in part of a cornflake packet or something similar.

FILING BOXES

Cover with smart plain paper, add a cut out reference card, and build up your own filing system. Shoe boxes are especially good for this.

PLASTIC TRAYS, DISHES AND TUBS

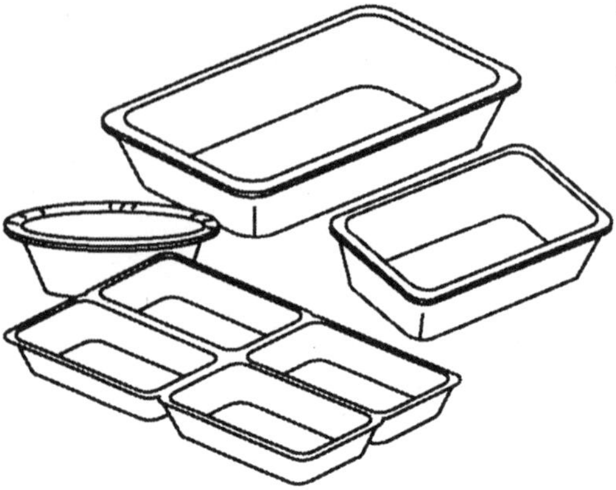

Margarine, ice cream, meat, fish, cakes, exotic fruits...there is an ever-increasing variety of opaque and clear plastic tubs, trays and dishes used in food packaging. These can be incredibly useful – particularly for culinary purposes that don't involve direct heat. So next time you're about to dump the packaging in the bin – don't! Build up a stock of shapes and sizes and think about the following possible uses...

Take advantage of the lidded tubs to eliminate the need for clingfilm or for buying purpose-designed products, by using them as:

MARINADING CONTAINERS

FREEZER STORAGE BOXES

The smaller, space-saving tubs, can be very useful for single portions.

CONTAINERS FOR LEFTOVERS

Useful for any food and particularly the contents of half empty cans, which should be transferred once opened.

SANDWICH BOXES

FLOURING BOXES

To coat fish or meat with seasoned flour, all you need to do is put it in a tub with the flour and shake.

PLANT POT UNDERTRAYS

Foamed polystyrene meat, fish, and vegetable trays are ideal for standing large plants and potted seedlings on. They're waterproof, won't scratch and will keep your window sills clean.

STERILISING TUBS

Bringing up children is expensive enough even without the long list of 'essential' equipment. A deep ice cream tub is ideal for baby equipment such as bottles, teats, dummies, etc, or anything else that might need sterilising. To keep the items submerged in the sterilising fluid, make an inner perforated plate by cutting a few holes in another lid and trimming it so that it will fit loosely inside the tub. Cover everything with the tub lid and soak items for the time specified by the sterilising solution manufacturer.

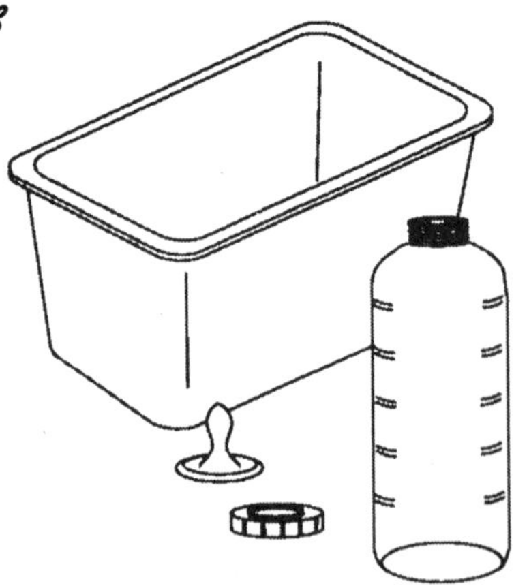

Other uses for tubs and trays include...

CLOTHES PEG HOLDERS

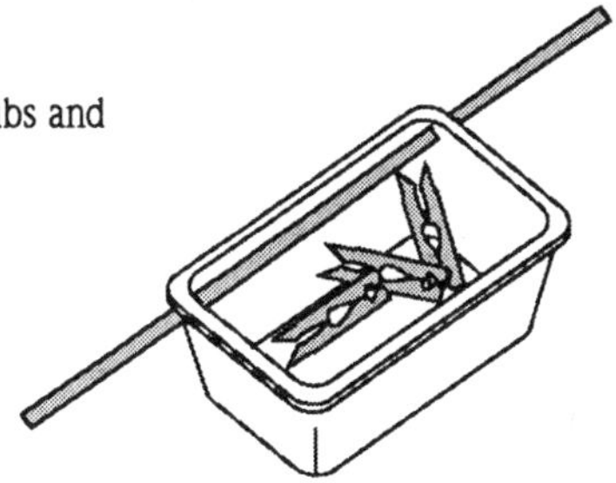

Large ice cream tubs make good peg holders – with their high firm sides, unlike a floppy bag, there is no 'fishing around' inside trying to get hold of the pegs, and they're easy to store on a shelf. It's very quick to attach a tub to your line and slide it along as you hang up the washing.

Cut two small holes, right in the back corner of the tub, on the two smaller sides. These should be slightly larger than the diameter of the line (see diagram). From the front edge of each hole make a 2 cm vertical cut downwards and join the bottom of these cuts together with a long horizontal cut across the back. Hang the tub by inserting the line under the resulting flap so that it rests in the two holes.

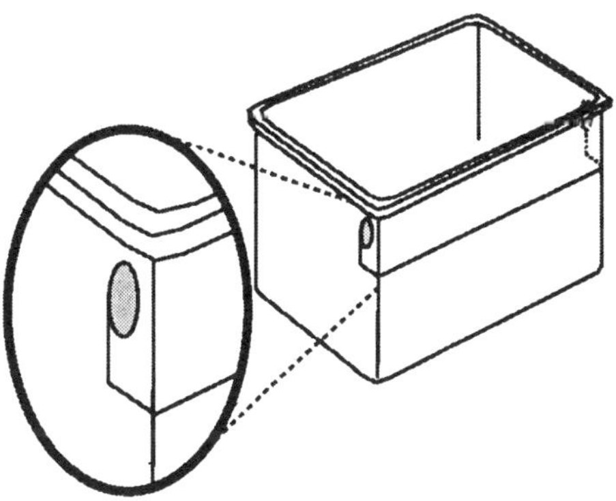

SEED TRAYS

STORAGE

Pins, buttons and paperclips – anything that is small and easily lost can be stored, stacked and kept tidy in margarine, ice cream tubs, etc.

BUG BOXES

Lightweight plastic tubs make perfect grasshopper and bug collecting boxes.

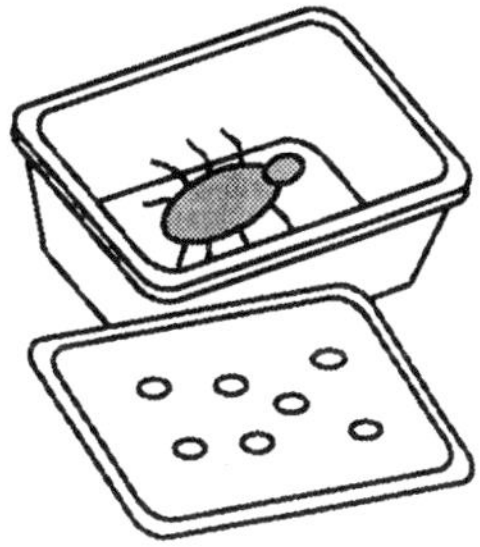

Don't forget to pierce some small airholes in the lid!

MICROWAVE DISHES

Most margarine tubs are made of polypropylene or ABS (acrlylonitrile butadiene styrene) which is the same material that microwave trays are made from. They can often be used in your microwave, but try a sample first as some may warp with hot fat. Follow your microwave manufacturer's instructions for testing the suitability of containers. Microwave ready-meal trays can also be reused of course.

PET FEEDING DISHES

FISHING BAIT BOXES

PAPER AND PLASTIC BAGS AND SACKS

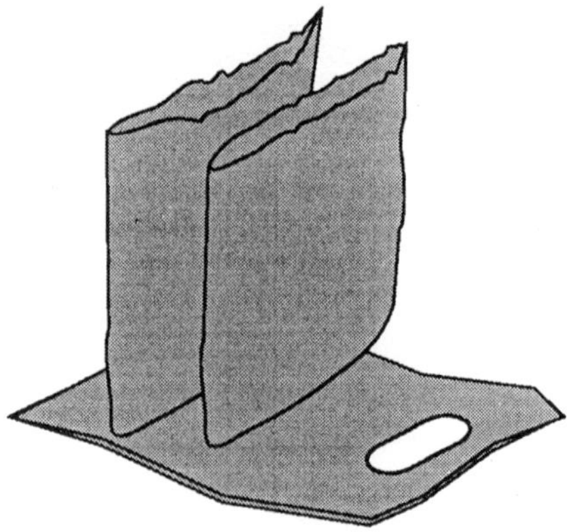

Once upon a time people washed out polythene bags and hung them up on the line to dry and use again. Now when so many things are put in them – do we really need to buy more for sandwich bags, freezer bags and rubbish bags? Save time and money – and help save the environment too – by reusing bags for...

FOOD WRAPPING

Do you really need to use clingfilm?

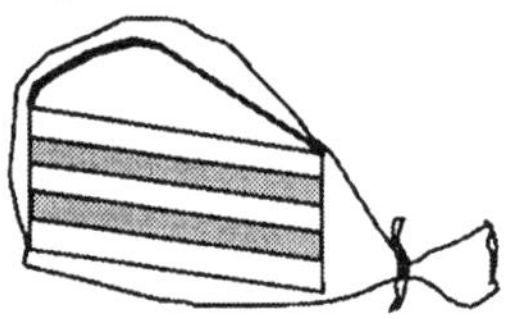

DOUGH BAGS

Remember bread dough will rest and rise just as well in an oiled bag as in a covered bowl.

ICING BAGS

Snip the corner off a clean plastic bag, insert the nozzle and you have a disposable icing bag.

FOOD FLOURING BAGS

Wash the meat or fish and then put it in a bag. Add the flour and seasoning and gently shake up and down.

This saves on the washing up and stops your hands from getting gooey!

CAR LITTER BAGS

A must if you arrive at the end of a journey in a welter of crisp packets, used tissues and other unmentionables! Save yourself time clearing out the car by using a rubber suction hook (obtainable from most hardware stores) to hang a suitable bag onto the back of the seat, car door or window.

BIN LINERS

Cut up and opened out large plastic bags can also be used for:

PICNIC TABLECLOTHS

PICNIC SEATS

COVERING SURFACES FOR 'CREATIVE' PLAY/FOOD PREPARATION

Last but not least – don't forget to save those carrier bags for shopping again, and for storing recycling materials.

DETERGENT AND BLEACH BOTTLES

A very large number of containers indeed come under the general description of household cleaning and toiletries products – so many in fact that a whole book could be written on them alone. This section and the next three cover the basic types – all in plastic – that most of us come across.

Use the conical top and straight sides of detergent and bleach bottles for...

PLANT WATERING MISERS

Cut funnels from the conical top part and remove any narrow neck piece. Wash out well and bury in the soil, pointing towards the roots. Fill with water and leave to soak. This saves you time – and all the water goes direct to your plants.

PLANT LABELS

Cut strips and mark the unprinted side with felt tips.

The easiest and quickest way to produce lots of labels is to cut the bottle into a cylinder and then cut lengthwise into strips.

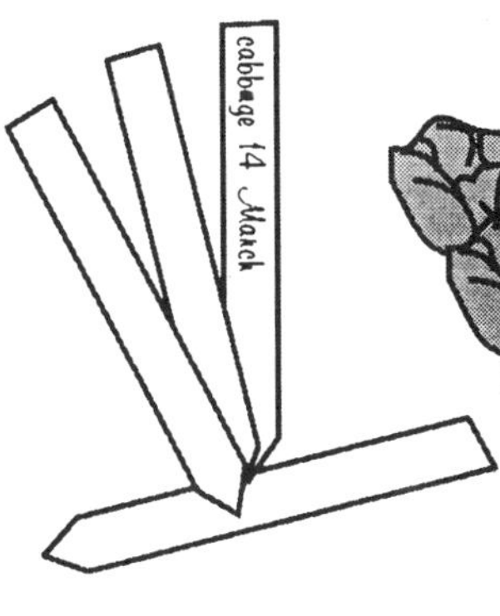

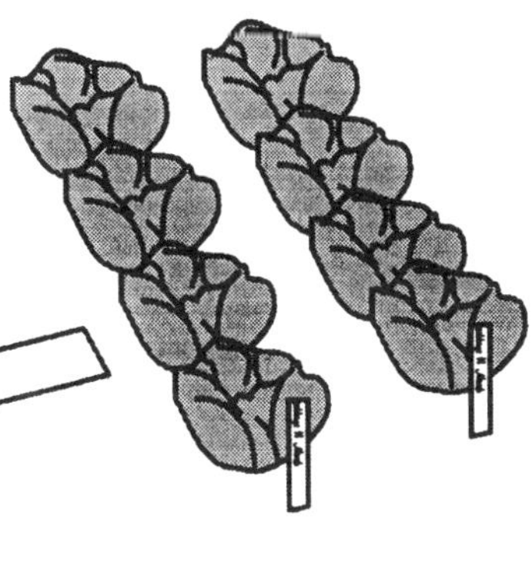

Remember that the squeezable, squirtable properties of bottles, such as those for washing-up liquid, can also be put to use as...

CHILDREN'S WATER SQUIRTERS

Children love to use suitable bottles for squirting (each other!) or watering the plants.

POSTER PAINT CONTAINERS

Ideal for keeping mixed powder paints ready for use.

SULPHUR/ CHEMICAL DUSTERS

Wash thoroughly, dry and fill with sulphur, fungicide, etc, and use as a blow duster. This saves a lot of time controlling moulds and pests on your fruit bushes, roses and other plants. Be sure to follow manufacturer's instructions regarding ventilation and safety, and label clearly.

LIQUID CLOTHES WASH BOTTLES

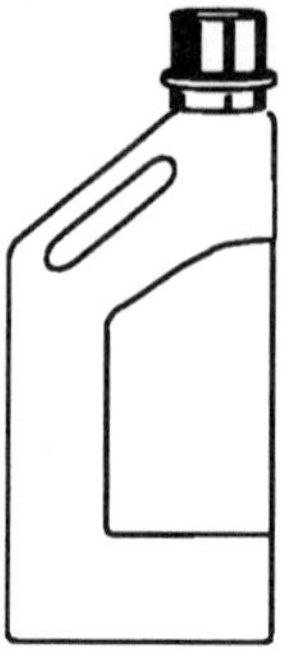

These containers have two properties which are very useful. Firstly, they're often quite large, straight-sided containers which provide good-sized sheets of plastic when cut up, and secondly, the material is quite thick by packaging standards, making it particularly suitable for fashioning simple items where strength is important.

With the body of the container...

CARRIER BAG TIDIES

Cut out a hole about 6cm high at the bottom of the bottle on the handle side (as shown). Remove cap and inner pourer and then stand on a shelf or fix to a wall, or inside a door (double-sided sticky pads are ideal for this). Push carrier bags in at the neck and pull them out at the bottom.

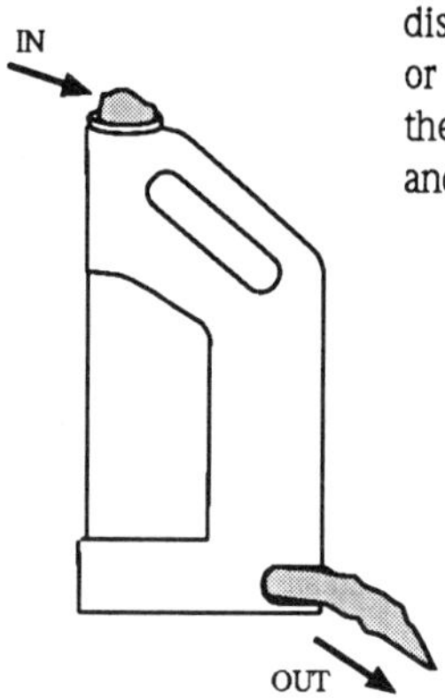

TOMATO PLANT FEED DISPENSERS

Save time mixing up feed. Using the cap, fill with the number of capfuls of water as are there measures stated on the feed packet. (Divide as appropriate if the bottle is not big enough for this number of capfuls.) Add all of the feed and dissolve. To use, simply pour one capful or (one-half if you divided by two) into the size of watering can recommended and top up with water.

TOY MEGAPHONES

Prise out the pouring spout and cut off the bottom. Hold with the handle and speak through the neck. Free, fun and reasonably effective – if unusually shaped!

LARGE FLOWER POTS

Cut off the bottom and pierce some drainage holes. Plants are not very fussy about the shape of the container as long as it's big enough.

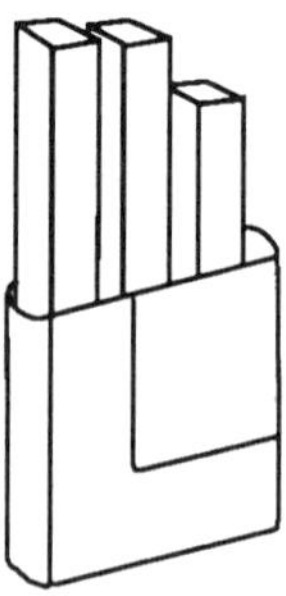

CLINGFILM/FOIL HOLDERS

The bottom of a large bottle is an ideal size to hold clingfilm, foil and other boxes. You can also use it as a space saver for items like polish, spices, etc. Screw, nail or stick with double-sided sticky pads to the insides of cupboards. To gain the maximum depth, cut as close to the bottom of the handle as possible.

Use bottle caps for...

BISCUIT CUTTERS

BATH/SANDPIT TOYS

PAINTBRUSH/ PENCIL POTS

SEEDLING POTS

DICE SHAKERS

MILK BOTTLE TOP COVERS

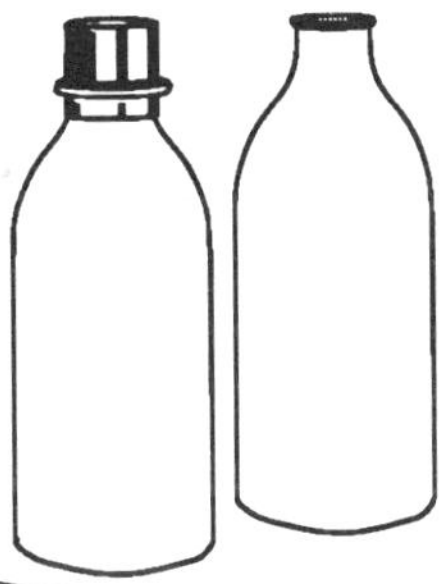

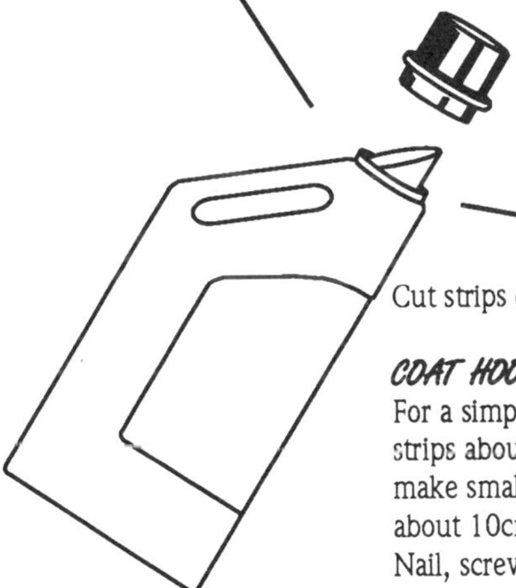

Cut strips of plastic to make...

COAT HOOKS

For a simple coat hook cut strips about 5cm wide and make small crescent cuts about 10cm apart as shown. Nail, screw or stick the strip to the inside of cupboards, or wherever required.

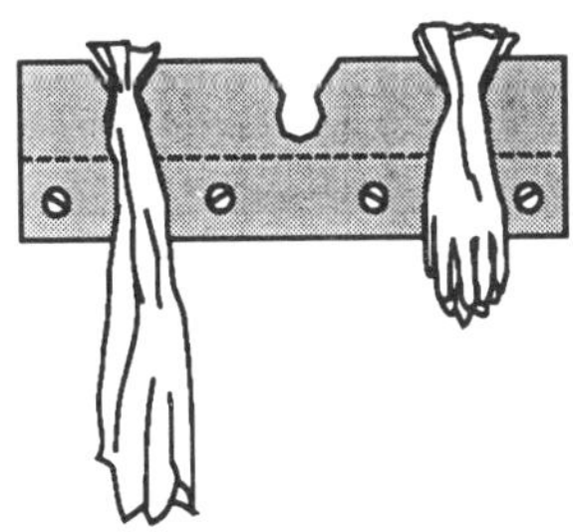

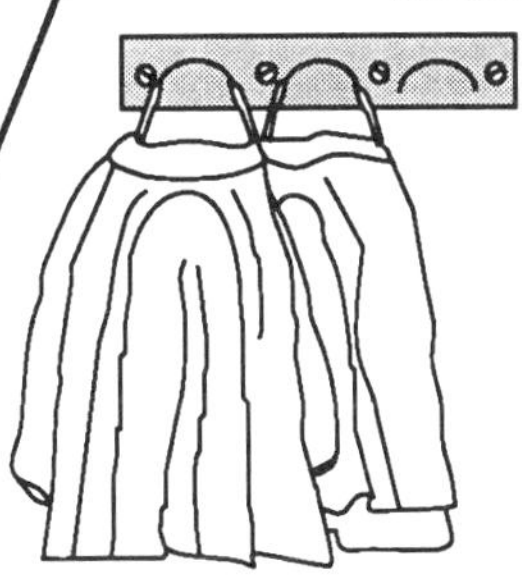

RUBBER GLOVE AND DUSTER HOLDERS

Cut up the plastic into strips, again about 6cm wide, with notches to grip gloves, dusters, and dishcloths. Nail, screw or stick to the inside of cupboards, or wherever required.

TOILETRIES AND CLEANING PRODUCT BOTTLES

Shampoo, hair conditioner, floor cleaner, polish, bubble bath...there are endless varieties of these containers, most of which are variations on a theme, designed to enchant the eye, have brand appeal, and be easy to use. Many have specific curves and grips moulded in for easier handling; different types of spouts, pourers and stoppers to dispense liquids, gels and powders; and snap close, childproof caps. Children love to reuse the shampoo and bubble bath bottles which are moulded as their favourite cartoon characters for...

MONEY BOXES

Cut a slot as near to the top as you can to make a child's money box which can be emptied through the neck or cut open when full.

PENCIL HOLDERS

Cut off the top of a suitable container to make an instant fun pencil holder.

Most of these containers – especially shampoo and cleaning product bottles — are made from thick plastic in various designs and sizes. Once they have been thoroughly washed out children enjoy using them as toys in the sandpit or in the bath. Or you can cut them up and make excellent...

PLAYDOUGH CUTTERS

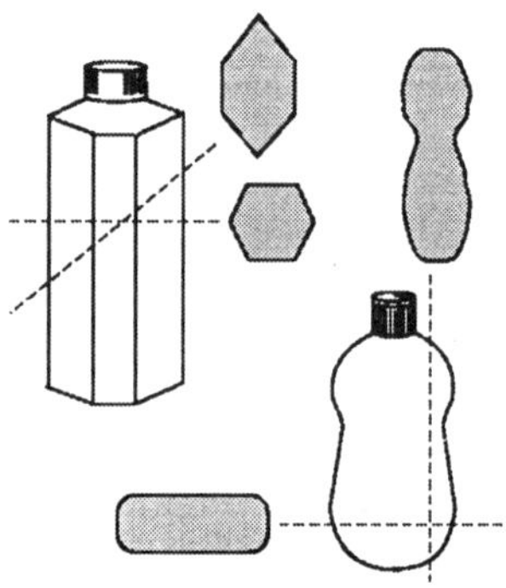

Use several different-shaped bottles made of thick plastic to produce shaped playdough cutters. Cutting a ring of material about 3cm deep works best. Make sure you smooth off all the jagged edges.

PLASTIC BAG CLIPS

Lots of these can be made from one bottle to keep handy for whenever you need something to reseal a plastic bag. Cut strips 2-3cm wide with a notch at one end as indicated in the diagram. Tightly wind up the neck of a bag and push into the notch. Longer clips can also be written on with felt tip pens to label the bags' contents.

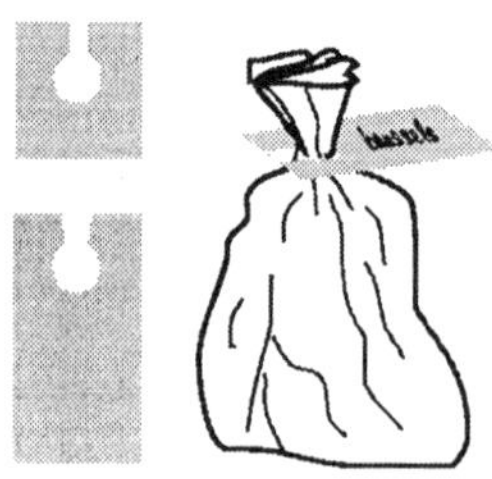

CARRIER BAG HAND PROTECTORS

These are a really effective way of stopping the handles of heavy plastic carrier bags from cutting into your hands. Cut a U-shaped section from the edge of a straightish-sided bottle, about 10cm long (for adult hands) and 4cm deep. Bend into a square profile as indicated at A with the top edge overlapping the bottom one. To use, slot the carrier bag handle into the protector. The handles of several bags can be held together in one protector, which also stops the bags from falling about when you put them down. Take a couple with you next time you go shopping and you'll be pleasantly surprised at the difference they'll make.

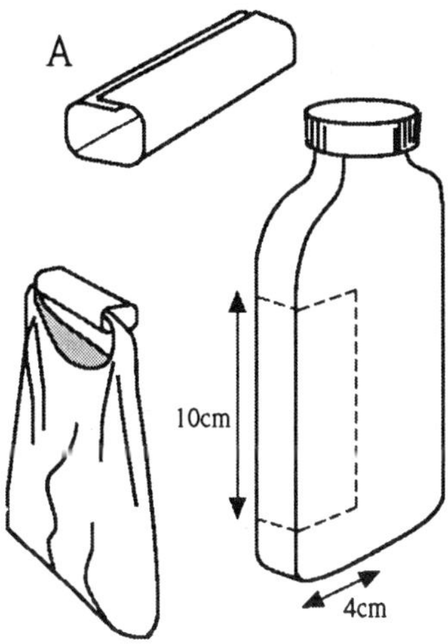

HANGING BASKET WATERERS

To ensure your flowers don't wilt if you are away for a couple of days, make a water store from a flatish shampoo bottle. Cut off the bottom and push the bottle upside-down into the compost, leaving the cap a little loose and fill with water. The water should be absorbed into the basket over a day or two. Tighten the cap if the flow is too fast. The larger the bottle the longer you can leave it.

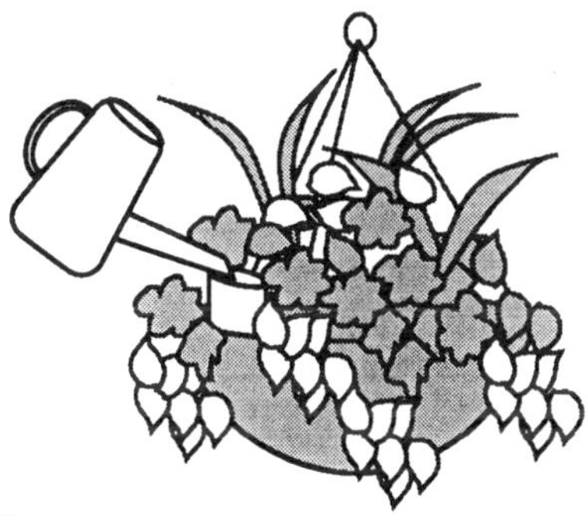

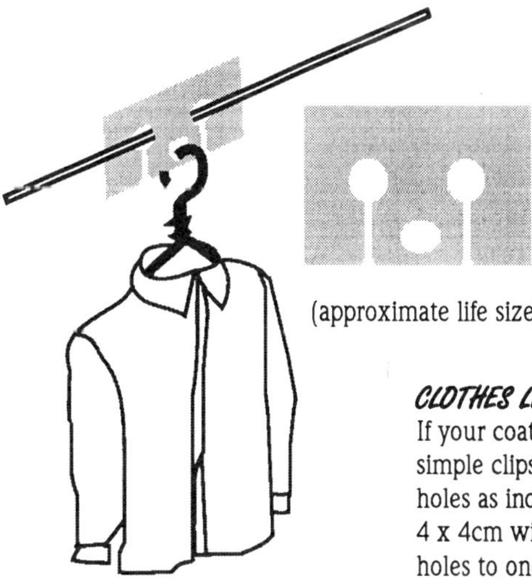

(approximate life size)

CLOTHES LINE CLIPS

If your coat hangers keep blowing off the line, these simple clips will help solve the problem. Cut three holes as indicated on a square piece of plastic about 4 x 4cm with two cuts joining the two adjacent holes to one edge. Hook over the line and insert the clothes hanger into the middle hole.

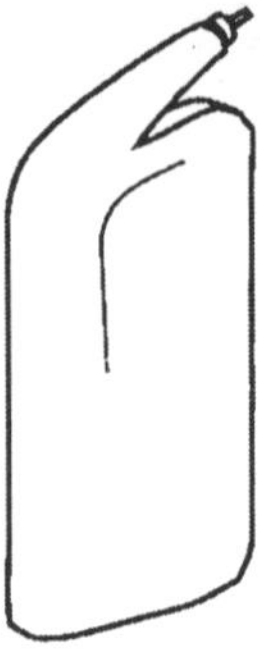

TOILET CLEANER DUCKS

Toilet cleaner ducks can be cut up and used in the same way as other cleaning product bottles but their bent necks and spouts make them particularly valuable for dispensing liquids in a fine stream or in drops – that's what they're designed for after all. The spout can be prised out for thorough cleaning and refilling for uses such as...

PLANT WATERING/ FEEDING

The angled spout makes watering pot plants, hanging baskets, etc, easy, and avoids spillage.

CLEANING SOLVENT DISPENSERS

Soapy water, soda solutions, – many non-toxic solutions and solvents are used for cleaning around the house, in the workshop and garden. Ducks are a convenient way to keep them instantly available for jobs like spots on the carpet, cleaning sparking plugs, grease on clothes – all the occasions when you need something available quickly with the minimum of effort. Remember to clean the toilet ducks out thoroughly first, label clearly, and store well out of children's reach.

OIL CANS

Fill one with some spare engine oil and keep handy for lubricating bikes, lawnmowers, tools, gates – and for all those times in the workshop and around the house when you need a drop of oil.

GLUE POTS

Water and solvent-based pastes and glues can be kept mixed up and dispensed easily using a 'duck'. Schools and playgroups, and anyone else who uses a lot of pastes and glues, will find this particularly useful.

CANS

Cans are awkward to reuse – requiring rather more in the way of tools to cut and work. Tin cans, particularly, provide a ready supply of steel sheet which can be used to fashion a great variety of craft items – but that is beyond the scope of this book. We have restricted this section to a few simple uses for both tin and drinks cans.

Of course, everybody has seen strings of cans behind the wedding car to provide a suitably rousing send off for the bride and groom! But reusing cans needn't stop at that...

Large tin cans are particularly useful for...

PAINTBRUSH SOAKING

PAINT KETTLES

Pierce two holes in the sides and attach a piece of bent wire coat hanger as a handle. Remember that to stop getting paint all over the kettle, professionals squeeze excess paint from the brush on the side of the kettle, rather than scraping it off on the edge.

WORKSHOP STORAGE

Strong, clean cans are ideal for keeping nuts and bolts, screws, spark plugs, washers and other bits and pieces safe, while working on the car, bike or boat. Make sure all the edges are smoothed off carefully.

Any size of can is ideal for...

GARDENING CANE COVERS

Every year there are serious accidents from plant supports and canes poking into eyes and faces when people bend down to tend to their plants. A can on each cane will not only make them safe but will also rattle and flash in the wind, helping to frighten off birds.

FLOWER POTS

If you are short of other containers for flower pots, aluminium drinks cans with the tops cut off are suitable as they won't rust or react with water or the wet compost/soil.

PASTRY CUTTERS

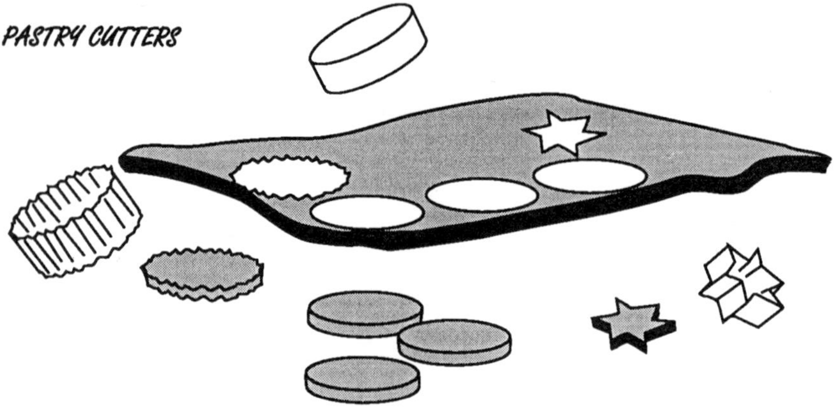

Make a variety of shapes and sizes of pastry and biscuit cutters by using the open end of any empty can (including drinks cans with the tops cut off) and by bending rings cut from the cans. To cut tin cans you will need a pair of tin snips; most drinks cans, however, can be cut with good, strong kitchen scissors. Cut rings about 2cm deep and mark out the required shape and size on a sheet of paper to follow as a template before bending the can with pliers. The edges will be very sharp so be careful – and smooth them off with a file, oilstone or fine emery paper. Wash well before use to remove any fragments of metal.

BIRD SCARING RATTLES

Make use of the 'going away car' technique – suspended strings of cans, each held in position by a knot on the string so that they just touch, will rattle and flash in the wind, helping to stop the birds from eating your crops. Pierce holes in the can bottoms, tie a knot at the bottom of the string and thread on the first can open end downwards. Continue up the string, measuring the position for each knot so that the cans just touch.

TOY INTERCOMS

Children have great fun using these. Pierce small holes in the bottom of two empty cans. (The easiest way of doing this is by placing the can base over a block of wood and using the point of a nail, struck hard with a hammer.) Thread a piece of string of the required length through both cans and knot at the ends. Stretch the string between the cans and take it in turns to talk to each other by speaking into one can and listening in the other. The string can be as long as you like but it has to be stretched taut with no obstructions, to make it work.

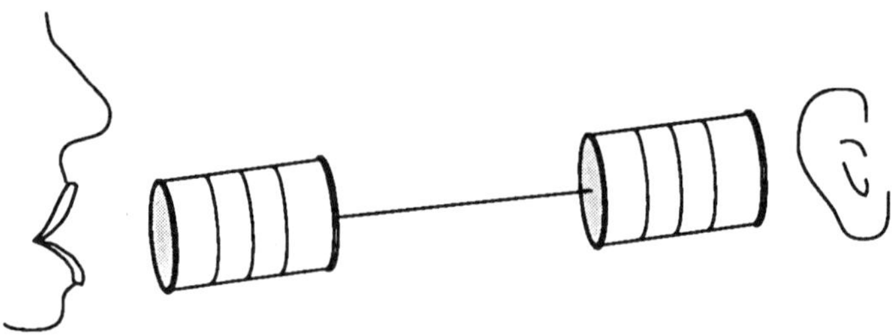

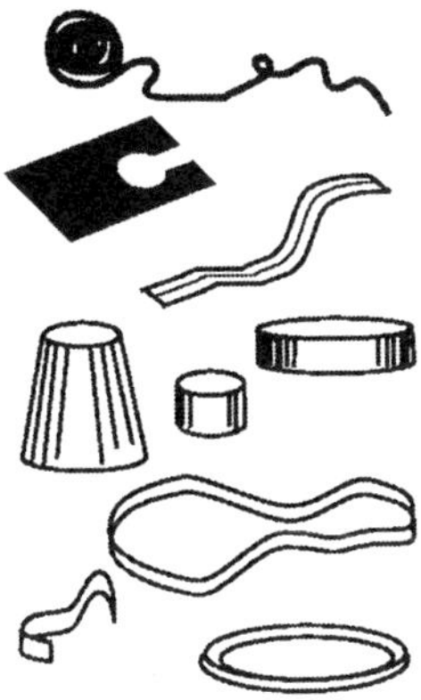

ODDS AND ENDS - TIES, CLOSURES AND LIDS

String, wire-strengthened plastic strips, caps and lids – there is an immense variety of odds and ends used to close and seal up packaging. They are usually a very small but essential part of any container. Most of us throw them away without a second thought but there are ways to reuse these too.
It was once said that the mark of a true English lady was that she never threw out bits of string and brown paper but carefully put then away for another day. Whether this definition is true or not, the principle is surely the ultimate test of the skilled and resourceful reuser!

Save plastic bag clips from supermarket fruit and vegetables for closing other bags for the freezer, sandwiches, bags of rice, pasta, etc. String, elastic bands and wire-reinforced plastic and paper strips can be similarly reused for things like...

GARDENING PLANT TIES

MEAT AND POULTRY TRUSSING

CLOSING PARCELS AND JIFFY BAGS

TYING BUNCHES OF FLOWERS AND VEGETABLES

Suitable caps and lids make great...

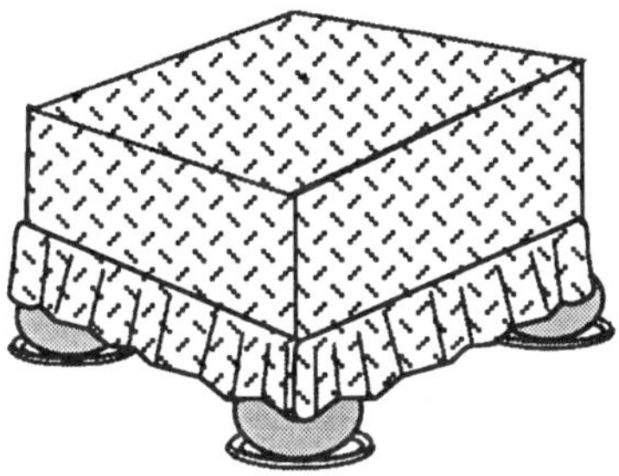

FURNITURE FEET GUARDS
Plastic jamjar lids are ideal for protecting carpets from furniture legs and castors.

PLANT POT COASTERS

DOOR STOPS
A plastic lid or cap – or several, placed one inside the other – can be screwed to a door, the floor or wall to make a free and effective door stop.

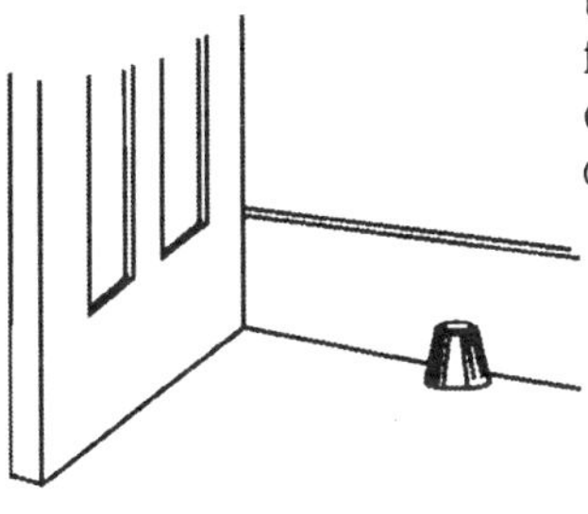

EGG CUPS
Use the conical tops of glass squash bottles for free egg cups.

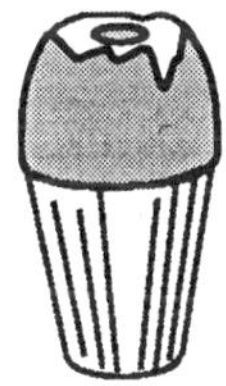

Make a collection of bits and pieces that look promising; plastic caps and lids, for instance, make very good wheels for homemade toys. Once you've started you'll be surprised at how often you'll find uses for them. Start to add your own to the ones above.

AND FINALLY – REUSE 251!

This book concentrates on 250 simple, practical ways to reuse packaging – quick and easy things that most people can do to get better value for money from something they've paid for. Two hundred and fifty ways is really quite a lot but there'd be something missing if we didn't remember the two hundred and fifty first:

if you can't think of anything else to do with it...

RECYCLE IT!

Remember too, that when you've finished using any packaging items, such as those described in this book, they can often be recycled afterwards. In fact many other 'waste' materials can be recycled besides packaging. Your local authority will have information on the range of facilities near you.

In the coming years more and more plastic containers will carry a symbol to tell you what they are made of and that they are recyclable, such as:

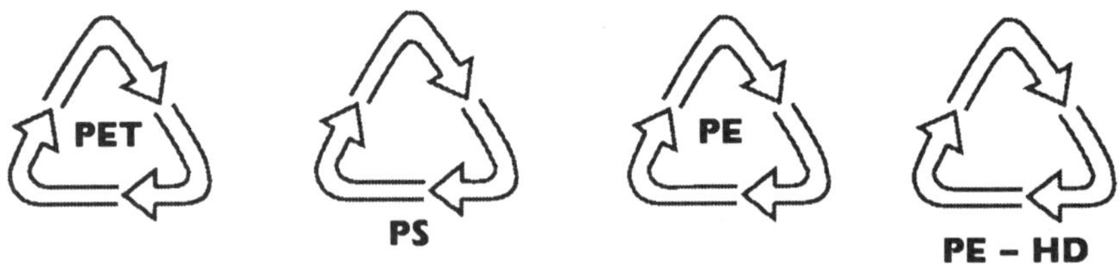

These four are for polyethylene terephthalate, polystyrene, polyethylene, and high-density polyethylene respectively. The symbols will make sorting easier, helping to reduce the cost of plastics recycling. Plastics account for a large and growing proportion of all packaging these days so increasing the reuse and recycling of the containers is very important.

Finally, do remember that schools and playgroups always need lots of containers for play and craft work, so don't forget them in your drive to reuse packaging!